D0880797

# Social Issues
## in Literature

# The Environment
# in Rachel Carson's
# *Silent Spring*

# Other Books in the Social Issues in Literature Series:

# Social Issues in Literature

# The Environment in Rachel Carson's *Silent Spring*

*Gary Wiener, Book Editor*

**GREENHAVEN PRESS**
*A part of Gale, Cengage Learning*

GALE
CENGAGE Learning

Detroit • New York • San Francisco • New Haven, Conn • Waterville, Maine • London

Elizabeth Des Chenes, *Managing Editor*

© 2012 Greenhaven Press, a part of Gale, Cengage Learning

Gale and Greenhaven Press are registered trademarks used herein under license.

*For more information, contact:*
Greenhaven Press
27500 Drake Rd.
Farmington Hills, MI 48331-3535
Or you can visit our Internet site at gale.cengage.com

For product information and technology assistance, contact us at

Gale Customer Support, 1-800-877-4253
For permission to use material from this text or product, submit all requests online at www.cengage.com/permissions

Further permissions questions can be emailed to permissionrequest@cengage.com

Articles in Greenhaven Press anthologies are often edited for length to meet page requirements. In addition, original titles of these works are changed to clearly present the main thesis and to explicitly indicate the author's opinion. Every effort is made to ensure that Greenhaven Press accurately reflects the original intent of the authors. Every effort has been made to trace the owners of copyrighted material.

Cover image copyright © Underwood & Underwood/Corbis.

**LIBRARY OF CONGRESS CATALOGING-IN-PUBLICATION DATA**

The environment in Rachel Carson's Silent spring. / Gary Wiener, book editor.
  p. cm. -- (Social issues in literature)
Summary: "Background on Rachel Carson; The Environment in Silent Spring; Contemporary Perspectives on the Environment"-- Provided by publisher.
  Includes bibliographical references and index.
  ISBN 978-0-7377-5815-3 -- ISBN 978-0-7377-5816-0 (pbk.)
  1. Carson, Rachel, 1907-1964. Silent Spring. 2. Environmental literature--History and criticism. 3. Environmental protection in literature. 4. Pesticides--Environmental aspects. 5. Pesticides--Toxicology. 6. Pesticides and wildlife. 7. Insect pests--Biological control. I. Wiener, Gary.
  QH545.P4E47 2011
  363.738'498--dc23
                                                                    2011038307

Printed in Mexico
1 2 3 4 5 6 7 15 14 13 12 11

# Contents

## Chapter 1: Background on Rachel Carson

## Chapter 2: The Environment in *Silent Spring*

An overlooked aspect of *Silent Spring* is the high quality of the writing itself. Carson uses techniques from science fiction and apocalyptic literature to lend power to her tale.

# Introduction

"To be great is to be misunderstood," wrote Ralph Waldo Emerson.[1] If his criterion for greatness is correct, then Rachel Carson must be counted among twentieth-century America's great writers and thinkers. Few books have ever been more misunderstood, deliberately misinterpreted, and scurrilously attacked than Carson's *Silent Spring*. Conversely, few books have ever been so revered as the one that many observers credit with having started the modern environmental movement. What Carson said in *Silent Spring*—and what she did not say—launched a heated debate that continues to this day. Nevertheless, Carson stands as a beacon of environmental light. As former vice president Al Gore wrote of Carson in his introduction to the 1994 edition of *Silent Spring*, "Her work, the truth she brought to light, the science and research she inspired, stand not only as powerful arguments for limiting the use of pesticides but as powerful proof of the difference that one individual can make."[2]

One need look no further than Carson's opening chapter, the famous "Fable for Tomorrow," to understand why *Silent Spring* initiated such controversy. In this chapter Carson describes a lifeless town where no birds sing: "only silence lay over the fields and woods and marsh."[3] Detractors often trumpet how Carson's tale has not come true: in the twenty-first century, all across the United States, birds still sing. But, as many commentators have noted, the key word in Carson's chapter title is "fable," and skeptics miss this crucial idea. A fable is a short allegorical narrative that suggests a moral. "Allegorical" implies that the story is not to be taken literally but rather is to imply symbolically a larger truth. In the words of biographer Ellen Levine, "It was meant to be a tale with a moral, a series of images to drive, like a line of poetry, straight to the heart of the issue."[4] But it was not meant, Levine argues, as a strictly literal statement of fact. According to biographer Arlene R. Quaratiello, Carson's "Fable for Tomorrow" drew numerous objections from the scientific community.[5] Nevertheless, Carson left it in the book. As explained by author Frank Graham Jr., Carson realized that for *Silent Spring* to take root in the US consciousness, "her book must persuade as well as inform; it must synthesize scientific fact with the most profound sort of propaganda."[6]

A second point of contention over *Silent Spring* stems from the notion that Carson was absolutely opposed to any pesticide use. Biographers and historians have dismissed this as patently false. Yet this perception persists in writings of those who deny that DDT is harmful to this day. One such antagonist, Dennis T. Avery, former senior policy analyst for the US State Department, drew parallels in 2007 between Carson and Adolf Hitler:

> The absence of DDT has led to the needless deaths of at least 30 million people from malaria and yellow fever in the tropics. (Five times as many as Hitler killed in his concentration death camps, albeit inadvertently). Most of them were helpless African children.[7]

Scientists and other commentators have strongly refuted Avery's statement. Many of today's scientists have disputed whether DDT is the supposed malarial panacea that Carson's critics contend it is. They note, as did Carson in Chapter 16 of *Silent Spring*, that mosquitoes develop a resistance to DDT, rendering the pesticide impotent. But Avery's chief fault, according to scholars, is his deliberate misreading of *Silent Spring*, because, they maintain, Carson never advocated for the abolition of all pesticides. What she was protesting, they explain, was the indiscriminate use of such chemicals as a massive, easy fix, in lieu of investigating alternative and perhaps more effective ways to deal with insect infestation. On the subject of insect-borne diseases and pesticides, Carson declared:

No responsible person contends that insect-borne diseases should be ignored. The question that has now urgently presented itself is whether it is either wise or responsible to attack the problem by methods that are rapidly making it worse. The world has heard much of the triumphant war against disease through the control of insect vectors of infection, but it has heard little of the other side of the story— the defeats, the short-lived triumphs that now strongly support the alarming view that the insect enemy has been made actually stronger by our efforts.[8]

In his article "Not So Fast with the DDT," which appeared in the *American Scholar*, writer Reed Karaim contends that DDT proponents have greatly distorted both Carson's beliefs as well as the facts about DDT and malaria:

DDT probably does have a role to play in battling malaria; indeed, a few African nations use it right now. But the new-found enthusiasm for dichlorodiphenyltrichloroethane comes with a few hitches. The first is that the pro-DDT people largely ignore evidence that greater use of the pesticide might kill as many African babies as it could save. A second problem is that the insecticide's proponents, either willfully or through ignorance, misrepresent the extent and conditions of the malaria epidemic in sub-Saharan Africa. A third is that they grossly simplify the complexity of disease control in the African environment. A final problem might not be equal in significance to the others, but it should matter to anyone who sees enduring virtue in great writing: DDT's high priests are unfair to a subtle and beautiful book and the courageous woman who wrote it.[9]

Many commentators have pointed out that the DDT controversy and the pesticide industry's attacks on Carson have masked the fact that *Silent Spring* was not first and foremost intended to be a treatise against the chemical industry. They assert that it has been written off by its antagonists as "that DDT book," but supporters see *Silent Spring* as a global call for a more balanced attitude toward nature and a warning that humankind's unchecked attempts to beat nature into submission could lead to disaster. "'The control of nature,'" Carson famously wrote in *Silent Spring*, "is a phrase conceived in arrogance, born of the Neanderthal age of biology and philosophy, when it was supposed that nature exists for the convenience of man."[10] To view *Silent Spring*, therefore, as merely a book about pesticides, its supporters claim, is to reduce the majesty and importance of Carson's work. As Geoffrey Norman writes, "The book . . . was about the spraying and what it did to the birds and other creatures. But that does not begin to describe its scope or account for its impact. One might just as well say that Darwin wrote about turtles and the Pacific islands where they were found."[11] Norman goes on to say:

> What Carson did in *Silent Spring* was to introduce to the general imagination the concept of ecology: the way the natural world fit together, the pieces so tightly and inextricably bound that you could not isolate cause and effect. The consequences of any action rippled through the whole system, affecting everything and sometimes even changing the system itself. So when we poisoned gypsy moths with massive sprayings of DDT, we were, ultimately, poisoning ourselves.

Biographer Linda Lear agrees: "Carson's legacy has less to do with pesticides than with awakening of environmental consciousness," she asserts, adding that Carson "changed the way we look at nature. We now know we are a part of nature, and we can't damage it without it coming back to bite us."[13]

*Silent Spring* has become an iconic book in the battle over environmentalism, so much so that its supporters, usually from the left of the political spectrum, and its detractors, usually from the right, have both filed claims that Carson was either the patron saint of radical environmentalism or the fascist in a dress who singlehandedly executed malaria victims. Even about the facts of Carson's death, many, if not most, of Carson's biographers err. It is true that in the last years of her life Carson was suffering from both heart disease and cancer. But most accounts of her death cite cancer as the cause, when she actually died of heart disease. This error has occurred because it supports the environmental cause Carson championed more to say that she died of the same disease, cancer, that she warned a generation about in her book. Linda Lear, in her 1997 biography, *Rachel Carson: Witness for Nature*, writes of Carson's death: "Late in the afternoon, on Tuesday, April 14 1964, Rachel Carson suffered a coronary heart attack. She died just before sunset."[14] It is true that her breast cancer, which had metastasized to her brain by the time of her death, would have eventually led to her demise,[15] but she did not die of it. In fact, Carson herself expressed the hope that she would succumb to her heart ailment before the cancer took her. In a letter to her close friend and confidante Dorothy Freeman, Carson wrote, "as to the angina, in a way it is almost like a secret weapon against the grimmer foe [cancer]—so if it should take me quickly . . . remember this is the easier way for me."[16] Environmental writer Paul Hawken, discussing Carson's death, remarks, "Rachel's wish was granted, and she died of cardiac arrest."[17] Critics point out that when Carson's own supporters claim that she died of cancer, they are being as duplicitous as her antagonists and are purposely misstating the truth. As author John Hay says, "One characteristic that follows her life was her passion for the truth, no matter how far or deep she had to go to find it."[18] Carson herself, quoting Jean Rostand in the second chapter of *Silent Spring*, writes that the public has "the right to know," and that only then can people decide what to do.[19]

The English satirist Jonathan Swift observed, "When a true genius appears in this world, you may know him by this sign, that the dunces are all in confederacy against him." So it was that with the publication of *Silent Spring* in 1962, a veritable army of attackers rose up against a woman whose stated goal was to promote a practical attitude toward public health and the environment. Though her enemies attempted to refute her claims in *Silent Spring*, labeling the book "junk science" and threatening lawsuits, it has been noted as significant that no litigious action was ever brought against her or her book. "Anticipating the reaction of the chemical industry, she had compiled *Silent Spring* as one would a lawyer's brief, with no fewer than 55 pages of notes and a list of experts who had read and approved the manuscript," according to the National Resources Defense Council.[20] Carson's enemies would not have been able to prove in court that she was wrong. To this day, however, websites such as Rachelwaswrong.org continue to assail Carson and her book with accusations that her science was incorrect or that she has singlehandedly stoked the malaria epidemic. But as Carson herself warned, "As you listen to the present controversy about pesticides . . . ask yourself: Who speaks? And Why?"[21] Rachelwaswrong.org is produced by the Competitive Enterprise Institute (CEI), a conservative-libertarian think tank whose founder, Fred Smith, is a well-known climate change skeptic. CEI's donors, moreover, include a number of multinational chemical corporations, including Monsanto, the original producer of DDT.

The essays that follow explore how and why Carson became known as a pioneer for the modern environmental movement and why, to this day, she and her writings are so variously interpreted. The viewpoints tackle the continuing controversy over chemical agriculture and humankind's relationship to the natural world. Whether the viewpoint authors agree or disagree with Miss Carson, their commentary attests that *Silent Spring*'s impact on American and global thinking about the environment has been profound, and this characteristic has led many to rank *Silent Spring* with other monumental literary efforts—among them, Upton Sinclair's *The Jungle*, Darwin's *Origin of Species*, and Harriet Beecher Stowe's *Uncle Tom's Cabin*—that have caused readers to alter the way they think about their world.

# Notes

1. Ralph Waldo Emerson, "Self Reliance," in *Essays by Ralph Waldo Emerson: First and Second Series Complete in One Volume*. New York: Perennial Library, 1988, p. 41.
2. Introduction to *Silent Spring*, by Rachel Carson. New York: Houghton Mifflin, 1994. Reprinted in *Courage for the Earth: Writers, Scientists, and Activists Celebrate the Life and Writing of Rachel Carson*, ed. Peter Matthiessen. Boston: Houghton Mifflin, 2007, p. 78.
3. Rachel Carson, *Silent Spring*. New York: Houghton Mifflin, 2002, p. 2.
4. Ellen Levine, *Up Close: Rachel Carson*. New York: Viking, 2007, p. 177.
5. Arlene Quaratiello, *Rachel Carson*. Amherst, NY: Prometheus, 2010, p. 115.
6. Frank Graham Jr., *Since "Silent Spring."* Boston: Houghton Mifflin, 1970, p. 22.
7. Dennis T. Avery, "Rachel Carson and the Malaria Tragedy," *Canada Free Press*, April 13, 2007.
8. Rachel Carson, *Silent Spring*. New York: Houghton Mifflin, 2002, p. 256.
9. Reed Karaim, "Not So Fast with the DDT: Rachel Carson's Warnings Still Apply," *American Scholar*, vol. 74, no. 3, 2005.
10. Rachel Carson, *Silent Spring*. New York: Houghton Mifflin, 2002, p. 297.
11. Geoffrey Norman, "The Flight of Rachel Carson," in *DISCovering Authors*. Detroit: Gale, 2003.
12. Ibid.
13. Quoted in Bruce Watson, "Sounding the Alarm," *Biophile Magazine*. http://biophile.co.za.
14. Linda Lear, *Rachel Carson: Witness for Nature*. Boston: Mariner, 1997, p. 480.
15. Mark Hamilton Lytle, *The Gentle Subversive: Rachel Carson, "Silent Spring," and the Rise of the Environmental Movement*. New York: Oxford University Press, 2007, p. 190.
16. Rachel Carson, Dorothy Freeman, and Martha E. Freeman, *Always, Rachel: The Letters of Rachel Carson and Dorothy Freeman, 1952–1964*. Boston: Beacon Press, 1995, p. 542.
17. Paul Hawken, *Blessed Unrest: How the Largest Movement in the World Came into Being, and Why No One Saw It Coming*. New York: Viking, 2007, p. 57.
18. John Hay, "A Long View of Rachel Carson," in *Courage for the Earth: Writers, Scientists, and Activists Celebrate the Life and Writing of Rachel Carson*, ed. Peter Matthiessen. Boston: Houghton Mifflin, 2007, p. 106.
19. Rachel Carson, *Silent Spring*. New York: Houghton Mifflin, 2002, p. 13.
20. "The Story of *Silent Spring*," National Resources Defense Council, April 16, 1997. http://www.nrdc.org.
21. *Speaking of Earth: Environmental Speeches That Moved the World*, ed. Alon Tal. New Brunswick, NJ: Rutgers University Press, 2006, p. 13.

# Chronology

**1907**
Rachel Carson is born on May 27 in Springdale, Pennsylvania.

**1913**
Carson enters Springdale Grammar School.

**1918**
Carson's story "A Battle in the Clouds" is published in *St. Nicholas Magazine.*

**1925**
Carson graduates first in her class from Parnassus High School.

She enrolls at the Pennsylvania College for Women.

**1928**
Carson changes her major from English to biology.

**1929**
Carson graduates with a BA in biology.

She begins graduate work at Johns Hopkins University.

**1930**
Carson's family moves to Baltimore, Maryland.

**1931**
Carson begins teaching at the University of Maryland.

**1932**
Carson earns her MA in zoology from Johns Hopkins.

**1935**
Robert Warden Carson, the writer's father, dies.

**1936**

Carson begins government work as an aquatic biologist.

**1941**

*Under the Sea-Wind* is published.

**1942**

Carson moves to Chicago to work for the Fish and Wildlife Service.

**1943**

Carson moves back to Maryland after promotion to associate aquatic biologist in the Fish and Wildlife Service.

**1945**

Carson is promoted to aquatic biologist.

She serves as general editor of *Conservation in Action* pamphlets.

**1946**

Carson is promoted to information specialist in the Division of Information.

**1949**

Carson is promoted to biologist and serves as editor-in-chief for Fish and Wildlife Information Division.

**1950**

The *Yale Review* publishes "The Birth of an Island."

**1951**

Carson wins a Guggenheim Fellowship. *The Sea Around Us* is published.

**1952**

*Under the Sea-Wind* is republished and becomes a best seller.

Carson resigns from the Fish and Wildlife Service.

**1955**
*The Edge of the Sea* is published.

**1956**
*The Women's Home Companion* publishes "Help Your Child to Wonder."

**1957**
Carson adopts her grandnephew Roger Christie after the death of his mother.

**1958**
Maria Carson, the writer's mother, dies.

**1962**
The *New Yorker* publishes a serialized version of *Silent Spring*.

Publication of the complete book, *Silent Spring*, follows.

**1963**
*The Silent Spring of Rachel Carson* airs on CBS.

**1964**
Rachel Carson dies of a heart attack on April 14.

*A Sense of Wonder* is published.

**1970**
The Environmental Protection Agency (EPA) is formed.

**1980**
President Jimmy Carter posthumously awards Rachel Carson the Presidential Medal of Freedom.

**1981**
The US Postal Service issues a Rachel Carson stamp.

**2007**
The post office in Springdale, Pennsylvania, is renamed after Carson.

# Background on
# Rachel Carson

# The Life of Rachel Carson

*Tom Crawford*

*Tom Crawford contributed to* Notable Women Scientists, *a collection of biographical sketches of women who have made a name in the scientific world.*

*In the following viewpoint, Crawford presents an overview of the life of Rachel Carson, who he indicates is often credited with initiating the environmental movement in the United States. Crawford asserts that from her earliest years Carson wanted to be a writer and some of the works she produced during those early years were published. An influential college professor led her to a lifelong interest in biology, Crawford reports, and Carson combined her two loves, first in working for the federal government as a science writer and later as the author of books on marine biology. Crawford details how, moved to action by a letter from a friend describing the harmful effects of the pesticide known as DDT, Carson wrote her seminal work,* Silent Spring. *The book, Crawford declares, made Carson both famous and infamous and brought national attention to the problem of excessive pesticide use.*

Rachel Carson is considered one of America's finest science and nature writers. She is best known for her 1962 book, *Silent Spring*, which is often credited with beginning the environmental movement in the United States. The book focused on the uncontrolled and often indiscriminate use of pesticides, especially dichlorodiphenyltrichloroethane (commonly known as DDT), and the irreparable environmental damage caused by these chemicals. The public outcry Carson generated by the book motivated the U.S. Senate to form a committee to investigate pesticide use. Her eloquent testimony before the committee altered the views of many government officials and helped lead to the creation of the Environmental Protection Agency (EPA).

## Early Years

Rachel Louise Carson, the youngest of three children, was born on May 27, 1907, in Springdale, Pennsylvania, a small town twenty miles north of Pittsburgh. Her parents, Robert Warden and Maria McLean Carson, lived on 65 acres and kept cows, chickens, and horses. Although the land was not a true working farm, it had plenty of woods, animals, and streams, and here, near the shores of the Allegheny River, Carson learned about the interrelationship between the land and animals.

Carson's mother was the daughter of a Presbyterian minister, and she instilled in her a love of nature and taught her the intricacies of music, art, and literature. Carson's early life was one of isolation; she had few friends besides her cats, and she spent most of her time reading and pursuing the study of nature. She began writing poetry at age eight and published her first story, "A Battle in the Clouds," in *St. Nicholas* magazine [for children] at the age of 10. She later claimed that her professional writing career began at age eleven, when *St. Nicholas* paid her a little over three dollars for one of her essays.

## A Career in the Sciences

Carson planned to pursue a career as a writer when she received a four-year scholarship in 1925 from the Pennsylvania College for Women (now Chatham College) in Pittsburgh. Here she fell under the influence of [Professor] Mary Scott Skinker, whose freshman biology course altered her career plans. In the middle of her junior year, Carson switched her major from English to zoology, and in 1928 she graduated magna cum laude. "Biology has given me something to write about," she wrote to a friend, as quoted in *Carnegie* magazine. "I will try in my writing to make animals in the woods or waters, where they live, as alive to others as they are to me."

With Skinker's help, Carson obtained first a summer fellowship at the Marine Biology Laboratory at Woods Hole in Massachusetts and then a one-year scholarship from the Johns Hopkins University in Baltimore. While at Woods Hole over the summer, she saw the ocean for the first time and encountered her first exotic sea creatures, including sea anemones and sea urchins. At Johns Hopkins, she studied zoology and genetics. Graduate school did not proceed smoothly; she encountered financial problems and experimental difficulties but eventually managed to finish her highly detailed master's dissertation, "The Development of the Pronephoros during the Embryonic and Early Larval Life of the Catfish (*Inctalurus punctaltus*)." In June 1932, she received her master's degree.

## Carson Begins Her Writing Career

Carson was entering the job market at the height of the Great Depression. Her parents sold their Pennsylvania home and moved to Maryland to ease some of her financial burdens. She taught zoology at Johns Hopkins [University] during the summers and on a part-time basis at the University of Maryland during the regular school year. While she loved teaching, the meager salaries she earned were barely enough to sustain herself, and, in 1935, her financial situation became even more desperate when her father died unexpectedly, leaving her solely responsible for supporting her fragile mother.

Before beginning her graduate studies at Johns Hopkins, Carson had arranged an interview with Elmer Higgins, who was head of the Division of Scientific Inquiry at the U.S. Bureau of Fisheries. Carson wanted to discuss her job prospects in marine biology, and Higgins had been encouraging, though he then had little to offer. Carson contacted Higgins again at this time, and she discovered that he had an opening at the Bureau of Fisheries for a part-time science writer to work on radio scripts. The only obstacle was the civil service exam, which women were then discouraged from taking. Carson not only did well on the test, she outscored all other applicants. She went on to become only the second woman ever hired by the bureau for a permanent professional post.

At the Bureau of Fisheries, Carson wrote and edited a variety of government publications—everything from pamphlets on how to cook fish to professional scientific journals. She earned a reputation as a ruthless editor who would not tolerate inconsistencies, weak prose, or ambiguity. One of her early radio scripts was rejected by Higgins because he found it too "literary." He suggested that she submit the script in essay form to the *Atlantic Monthly*, then one of the nation's premier literary magazines. To Carson's amazement, the article was accepted and published as "Undersea" in 1937. Her jubilation over the article was tempered by personal family tragedy. Her older sister, Marian, died at age forty that same year, and Carson had to assume responsibility for Marian's children, Marjorie and Virginia Williams.

## Under the Sea-Wind

The *Atlantic Monthly* article attracted the notice of an editor at the publishing house of Simon & Schuster, who urged Carson to expand the four-page essay into book form. Working diligently in the evenings, she was able to complete the book in a few years; it was published as *Under the Sea-Wind*. Unfortunately, the book appeared in print in 1941, just one month before the Japanese attacked Pearl Harbor. Despite favorable, even laudatory reviews, it sold fewer than 1,600 copies after six years in print. It did, however, bring Carson to the attention of a number of key people, including the influential science writer William Beebe published an excerpt from *Under the Sea-Wind* in his 1944 compilation *The Book of Naturalists,* including Carson's work alongside the writings of Aristotle, Audubon, and Thoreau.

The poor sales of *Under the Sea-Wind* made Carson concentrate on her government job. The Bureau of Fisheries merged with the Biological Survey in 1940 and was reborn as the Fish and Wildlife Service. Carson quickly moved up the professional ranks, eventually reaching the position of biologist and chief editor after World War II. One of her postwar assignments, a booklet about National Wildlife Refuges called *Conservation in Action,* took her back into the field. As part of her research, she visited the Florida Everglades, Parker River in Massachusetts, and Chincoteague Island in the Chesapeake Bay.

## Carson Attracts National Notice

After the war, Carson began work on a new book that focused on oceanography. She was now at liberty to use previously classified government research data on oceanography, which included a number of technical and scientific breakthroughs. As part of her research, she did some undersea diving off the Florida coast during the summer of 1949. She battled skeptical administrators to arrange a deep-sea cruise to Georges Bank near Nova Scotia aboard the Fish and Wildlife Service's research vessel, the *Albatross III.*

Entitled *The Sea around Us,* her book on oceanography was published on July 2, 1951. It was an unexpected success; abridged in *Reader's Digest,* it was a Book-of-the-Month Club alternative selection and it remained on the *New York Times* bestseller list for 86 weeks. The book brought Carson numerous awards, including the National Book Award and the John Burroughs Medal, as well as honorary doctorates from her alma mater and Oberlin College. Despite her inherent shyness, Carson became a regular on the lecture circuit. Money was no longer the overarching concern it had been; she retired from government service and devoted her time to writing.

Freed from financial burdens, Carson began work on another book, focusing this time on the intricacies of life along the shoreline. She took excursions to the mangrove coasts of Florida and returned to one of her favorite locations, the rocky shores of Maine. She fell in love with the Maine coast and in 1953 bought a summer home in West Southport on the shore of Sheepscot Bay. *The Edge of the Sea* appeared in 1955 and earned Carson two more prestigious awards, the Achievement Award of the American Association of University Women and a citation from the National Council of Women of the United States. The book remained on the bestseller list for 20 weeks, and [film producers] RKO Studios bought the rights to it. In typical Hollywood fashion, the studio sensationalized the material and ignored scientific fact. Carson corrected some of the more egregious errors but still found the film embarrassing, even after it won an Oscar as the best full-length documentary of 1953.

From 1955 to 1957, Carson concentrated on smaller projects, including a telescript, "Something about the Sky," for the *Omnibus* series. She also contributed a number of articles to popular magazines. In July 1956, Carson published "Help Your Child to Wonder" in the *Woman's Home Companion*. The article was based on her own real-life experiences, something rare for Carson. She intended to expand the article into a book and retell the story of her early life on her parent's Pennsylvania farm. After her death, the essay reappeared in 1965 as the book *The Sense of Wonder*.

## Investigating Pesticide Use

In 1956, one of the nieces Carson had raised died at age 36. Marjorie left her son Roger; Carson now had to care for him in addition to her arthritic mother, who was now 88. She legally adopted Roger that same year and began looking for a suitable place to rear the child. She built a new winter home in Silver Spring, Maryland, on an uncultivated tract of land,

*Rachel Carson (1952).* © Hank Walker/Time & Life Pictures/Getty Images.

and she began another project shortly after the home was finished. The luxuriant setting inspired her to turn her thoughts to nature once again. Carson's next book grew out of a long-held concern about the overuse of pesticides. She had received a letter from [her friend] Olga Owens Huckins, who related how the aerial spraying of DDT had destroyed her Massachusetts bird sanctuary. Huckins asked her to petition federal authorities to investigate the widespread use of such pesticides, but Carson thought the most effective tactic would be to write an article for a popular magazine. When her initial queries were rejected, Carson attempted to interest the well-known essayist E. B. White in the subject. White suggested she write the article herself, in her own style, and he told her to contact William Shawn, an editor at the *New Yorker*. Eventually, after numerous discussions with Shawn and others, she decided to write a book instead.

## *Silent Spring* Sparks Controversy

The international reputation Carson now enjoyed enabled her to enlist the aid of an array of experts. She consulted with biologists, chemists, entomologists, and pathologists, spending four years gathering data for her book. When *Silent Spring* first appeared in serial form in the *New Yorker* in June 1962, it drew an aggressive response from the chemical industry. Carson argued that the environmental consequences of pesticide use underscored the futility of humanity's attempts to control nature, and she maintained that these efforts to assume control had upset nature's delicate balance. Although the message is now largely uncontroversial, the book caused near panic in some circles, challenging the long-held belief that humans could master nature. The chemical companies, in particular, attacked both the book and its author; they questioned the data, the interpretation of the data, and the author's scientific credentials. One early reviewer referred to Carson as a "hysterical woman," and others continued this sexist line of attack. Some chemical companies attempted to pressure Houghton Mifflin, the book's publisher, into suppressing the book, but these attempts failed.

The general reviews were much kinder and *Silent Spring* soon attracted a large, concerned audience, both in America and abroad. A special CBS television broadcast, "The Silent Spring of Rachel Carson," which aired on April 3, 1963, pitted Carson against a chemical company spokesman. Her cool-headed, commonsensical approach won her many fans and brought national attention to the problem of pesticide use. The book became a cultural icon and part of everyday household conversation. Carson received hundreds of invitations to speak, most of which she declined due to her deteriorating health. She did find the strength to appear before the Women's National Press Club, the National Parks Association, and the Ribicoff Committee—the U.S. Senate committee on environmental hazards.

## Honors and Death

In 1963 Carson received numerous honors and awards, including an award from the Izaak Walton League of America, the Audubon Medal, and the Cullen Medal of the American Geographical Society. That same year, she was elected to the prestigious American Academy of Arts and Sciences. She died of heart failure [she was also suffering from breast cancer] on April 14, 1964, at the age of 56. In 1980, President Jimmy Carter posthumously awarded her the President's Medal of Freedom. A Rachel Carson stamp was issued by the U.S. Postal Service in 1981.

# Rachel Carson Was a Hero

*Terry Tempest Williams*

*Terry Tempest Williams is an American author, naturalist, and conservationist. Her books include* Finding Beauty in a Broken World *and* The Open Space of Democracy.

*In the following viewpoint, environmentalist Williams writes about the impact of Rachel Carson on her own life and work, starting with the first time Williams heard her grandparents mention Carson's name. Williams asserts that Carson's books have had a profound impact on modern environmentalism and that Carson serves as a pioneer and role model for those who have followed in her path. Carson's struggles were numerous, Williams observes, and she displayed great courage in defending herself and her work against all those who sought to vilify her. Williams concludes that Carson's courage distinguishes her as a hero for today's environmental advocates.*

Rachel Carson. I first heard her name from my grandmother. I must have been seven or eight years old. We were feeding birds—song sparrows, goldfinches, and towhees—in my grandparents' yard in Salt Lake City, Utah.

"Imagine a world without birds," my grandmother said as she scattered seed and filled the feeders. "Imagine waking up to no birdsong."

I couldn't.

"Rachel Carson," I remember them saying.

Later, around the dinner table, she and my grandfather were engaged in an intense discussion of the book they were reading, *Silent Spring* as my mind tried to grasp what my grandmother had just said about a muted world.

Terry Tempest Williams, "Rachel Carson," *American Rebels*, edited by Jack Newfield, New York: Nation Books, 2003, pp. 343–354. Reproduced by permission of Perseus Books.

## Carson the Hero

Decades later, I found myself in a used bookstore in Salt Lake City. The green spine of *Silent Spring* caught my eye. I pulled the classic off the shelf and opened it. First edition, 1962. As I read various passages, I was struck by how little had changed. Each page was still a shock and a revelation:

> One of the most tragic examples of our unthinking bludgeoning of the landscape is to be seen in the sagebrush lands of the West, where a vast campaign is on to destroy the sage and to substitute grasslands. If ever an enterprise needed to be illuminated with a sense of history and meaning of the landscape, it is this. It is spread before us like the pages of an open book in which we can read why the land is what it is, and why we should preserve its integrity. But the pages lie unread.

The pages of abuse on the American landscape still lie unread.

Rachel Carson is a hero, a towering example within American democracy of how one person's voice can make an extraordinary difference both in public policy and in the minds of the populace. Her name and her vision of a world intact and interrelated has entered mainstream culture. We can all rattle off a glib two-sentence summation of its text: "All life is connected. Pesticides enter the food chain and not only threaten the environment but destroy it." And yet, I fear that *Silent Spring*'s status as "an American classic" allows us to nod to its power, but to miss the subtleties and richness of the book as both a scientific treatise and a piece of distinguished literary nonfiction.

## Carson as a Storyteller

Rachel Carson presents her discoveries of destruction in the form of storytelling. In example after example, grounded in the natural world, she weaves together facts and fictions into an environmental tale of life, love, and loss. Her voice is graceful and dignified, but sentence by sentence she delivers right hand blows and counter punches to the status quo ruled by chemical companies within the Kingdom of Agriculture:

> The 'control of nature' is a phrase conceived in arrogance, born of the Neanderthal age of biology and philosophy, when it was supposed that nature exists for the convenience of man it is our alarming misfortune that so primitive a science has armed itself with the most modern and terrible weapons, and that in turning them against the insects it has also turned them against the earth.

The facts she presents create the case against "biocide": We are killing the very fabric of nature in our attempt to rid the world of pests through these "elixirs of death." She indicts the insecticides by name: DDT, chlordane, heptachlor, dieldrin, aldrin, and endrin. And then adds to the toxic hydrocarbons, the alkyl or organic phosphates, among the most poisonous chemicals in the world: parathion and malathion.

The fictions she exposes are the myths we have chosen to adopt to our obsession to control nature. She reminds us of the story of Medea, the Greek sorceress who, overwrought with jealously over her husband's love of another woman, presents the new bride with a gift, a robe that will immediately kill whoever wears it. It becomes a garment of death. Carson calls our use of pesticides "death by indirection." We are killing insects and in turn, killing ourselves, as these toxins slowly and violently enter the waters and eventually our own bloodstreams. Rachel Carson did not turn her back from the ongoing chronicle of the natural history of the dead. She bore witness. "It was time," Carson said, "that human beings admit their kinship with other forms of life. If we cannot accept this moral ethic, then we too are complicit in the killing."

With each chapter, she adds to our understanding of the horrors of herbicides and hydrocarbons, the web of life unraveling. It is impossible for us not to be mindful of Rachel Carson's emotional and intellectual stamina, of her ability to endure the pain of the story she was telling.

But Miss Carson had a vision.

"Sometimes, I lose sight of my goal," she wrote in an essay in her first year of college. "Then again it flashes into view, filling me with a new determination to keep the vision before my eyes." Hers was a conscientious and directed soul who believed in the eloquence of facts. She loved both language and landscape. "I can remember no time when I wasn't interested in the out-of-doors and the whole world or nature," Carson said.

## Life Before *Silent Spring*

Writing became the expression of her passion toward nature. She published her first story when she was ten years old, winning the Silver Badge from the prestigious children's magazine, *St. Nicholas*. "Perhaps the early experience of seeing my work in print played its part in fostering my childhood dream of becoming a writer."

Here was a young woman already on her path. In 1928, she graduated magna cum laude from Pennsylvania College for Women, now Chatham College, with a major in zoology. The strength of her course work in both science and literature provides evidence of her dual nature as both a scientist and a poet. "I thought I had to be one of the other," she said. "It never occurred to me that I could combine two careers."

Rachel Carson's editor Paul Brooks writes, "The merging of these two powerful currents—the imagination and insight of a creative writer with a scientist's passion for fact—goes far to explain the blend of beauty and authority that was to make her books unique."

Perhaps this is Rachel Carson's greatest gift to us, seeing the world whole.

Carson continued her education as a biologist, receiving a master's degree in zoology at Johns Hopkins University, where she studied genetics. Her thesis, "The Development of the Pronephros During the Embryonic and Early Larval Life of the Catfish (*Inctalurus punctatus*)," should quell the ongoing criticism that Rachel Carson was merely an "amateur naturalist."

In 1936, she accepted a position with the United States Bureau of Fisheries, which later became the U.S. Fish and Wildlife Services, as an aquatic biologist. Here she was able to forcefully fuse her talents as a scientist and a writer, eventually becoming chief of publications for the bureau. Early in her tenure at Fish & Wildlife, she continued teaching at the University of Maryland and Johns Hopkins.

*Under the Sea-Wind* was published in 1941. *The Sea Around Us* was published in 1951 to great popular and critical acclaim, receiving the National Book Award in nonfiction. It remained on the *New York Times* bestsellers list for months. "If there is poetry in my book about the sea," she said, "it is not because I deliberately put it there, but because no one could truthfully write about the sea and leave out the poetry."

In 1955, four years after the success of *The Sea Around Us*, Carson published *The Edge of the Sea*, extending her readers' knowledge of the ocean to the ocean's interface with land. She brought her naturalist's eye down to the intricacies of tidepools and illuminated the habitats of the sandy beach and rocky shore.

## Carson Is Inspired to Write *Silent Spring*

And then came *Silent Spring*.

Rachel Carson received a burning letter from her friend Olga Owens Huckins, a journalist, who asked her for help in finding people who could elucidate and speak to the dangers of pesticides. The Huckinses had a small place in Duxbury, Massachusetts, just north of Cape Cod, which they had made into a bird sanctuary. Without any thought of the effects on birds and wildlife, the state had sprayed the entire area for mosquito control.

Huckins sent a letter of outrage to the *Boston Herald* in January, 1958. Here is an excerpt:

> The mosquito control plane flew over our small town last summer. Since we live close to the marshes, we were treated to several lethal doses as the pilot crisscrossed our place. And we consider the spraying of active poison over private land to be a serious aerial intrusion.
>
> The 'harmless' shower bath killed seven of our lovely songbirds outright. We picked up three dead bodies the next morning right by the door . . . . The next day three were scattered around the bird bath. (I had emptied it and scrubbed it after the spraying but YOU CAN NEVER KILL DDT).
>
> . . . All of these birds died horribly and in the same way. Their bills were gaping open, and their splayed claws were drawn up to their breasts in agony.

Olga Owens Huckins bore witness. Rachel Carson responded. Four and a half years later in 1962, *Silent Spring* was published. Carson wrote to Huckins that it was her letter that had "started it all" and had led her to realize that "I must write the book."

Rachel Carson told the truth as she understood it. The natural world was dying, poisoned by the hands of power tied to corporate greed. Her words became a catalyst for change. A debate had begun: a reverence for life versus a reverence for industry. Through the strength and vitality of her voice, Carson altered the political landscape of America.

Loren Eisely wrote that *Silent Spring* "is a devastating, heavily documented, relentless attack upon human carelessness, greed, and responsibility."

## Attacks on Carson's Credibility

Not everyone saw it that way.

The Monsanto Chemical Company, anticipating the publishing of *Silent Spring*, urgently commissioned a parody entitled "The Desolate Year" to counteract Carson's attack on the industry. Its intent was to show the pestilence and famine that the company claimed would occur in a world without pesticides.

Robert White-Stevens, the chemical industry's chief spokesman, made over twenty eight speeches against *Silent Spring*, charging that Carson was "a fanatic defender of the cult of the balance of nature."

In its weekly newsletter, the *American Medical Association* told the public how to obtain an "information kit," compiled by the National Agriculture Chemicals Association, to answer questions provoked by *Silent Spring*.

*Time* magazine called *Silent Spring* "unfair, one-sided, and hysterically over-emphatic," accused Carson of frightening the public with "emotion-fanning words," and claimed her text was filled with "oversimplifications and downright errors."

Former Secretary of Agriculture Ezra Taft Benson wrote to [President] Dwight D. Eisenhower regarding Rachel Carson, asking simply, "Why a spinster with no children was so concerned about genetics?" His own conjecture was that she was "probably a Communist."

Spinster. Communist. A member of a nature cult. An amateur naturalist who should stick to poetry not politics. These were just some of the labels used to discredit her. Rachel Carson had in fact, lit a fire on America's chemical landscape.

## Carson Fights Back

In speeches before the Garden Club of America and the New England Wildflower Preservation Society, Miss Carson fought back against her detractors and addressed her audiences with great passion, "I ask you to ask yourself—Who speaks?—And Why?" And then again, "Are we being sentimental when we care whether the robin returns to our dooryard and the veery sings in the twilight woods? A world that is no longer fit for wild plants, that is no longer graced by the flight of birds, a world whose streams and forests are empty and lifeless is not likely to be a fit habitat for man himself, for these things are symptoms of an ailing world."

President John F. Kennedy became aware of *Silent Spring* when it was first serialized in the pages of *The New Yorker*. At a press conference on August 29, 1962, a reporter asked Kennedy about the growing concern among scientists regarding dangerous long-term side effects from the use of DDT and other pesticides and whether or not the U.S. Department of Agriculture of the U.S. Public Health Service was planning to launch an investigation into the matter.

"Yes," the President replied. "I think particularly, of course, since Miss Carson's book."

The Life Sciences Panel of the President's Science Advisory Committee was charged with reviewing pesticide use. In 1962, the committee issued a call for legislative measures to safeguard the health of the land and its people against pesticides and industrial toxins. The President's report had vindicated Carson. Her poetics were transformed into public policy.

Rachel Carson testified for over forty minutes during the Hearings before the United States Senate Subcommittee on Reorganization and International Organizations of the Committee on Government Operations, "Interagency Coordination in Environmental Hazards (Pesticides)," on June 4, 1964.

According to Carson's biographer, Linda Lear, "Those who heard Rachel Carson that morning did not see a reserved or reticent woman in the witness chair but an accomplished scientist, an expert on chemical pesticides, a brilliant writer, and a woman of conscience who made the most of an opportunity few citizens of any rank can have to make their opinions known. Her witness had been equal to her vision."

Senator [Ernest] Gruening from Alaska called *Silent Spring* equal to *Uncle Tom's Cabin* [Harriet Beecher Stowe's novel about slavery] in its impact, and predicted it would change the course of history.

In 1967, five years after *Silent Spring* was published, the Environmental Defense Fund was born, with a mandate, in the words of one its founders, "to build a body of case law to establish a citizen's right to a clean environment." Three years after that, in 1970, the Environmental Protection Agency was established.

## Carson's Death

Rachel Carson died of breast cancer on April 14, 1964, at the age of 56. The irony is a painful one. Diagnosed in 1960, she wrote *Silent Spring* through her illness and faced her powerful detractors with limited physical strength, often having to be hospitalized after strenuous professional obligations. But the public never knew. She proceeded with great presence and resolve, even completing a rigorous television interview on CBS months before her death, where she was paired with a spokesperson from the chemical industry. Miss Carson's "grace under fire" with compelling facts to back her sentiments finally won public opinion over to her side. Brooks Atkinson in his column in the *New York Times* proclaimed her the winner. He wrote, "Evidence continues to accumulate that she is right and that *Silent Spring* is the 'rights of man' [referring to Thomas Paine's book] of this generation."

In spite of her cancer, Rachel Carson never lost "the vision splendid" before her eyes. Her love of the natural world, especially all she held dear in the coastal landscape of Maine, sustained her, giving her uncommon strength and peace.

Before her death, she wrote to her friend, E.B. White, "It is good to know that I shall live on even in the minds of many who do not know me and largely through association with things that are beautiful and lovely."

And she does.

## Carson's Legacy

Consider these examples: Rachel's Daughters, a film about the environmental causes of breast cancer; Rachel's Network, a political organization committed to seeing women in positions of power and leadership within the conservation community; And consider the thousands of references to Rachel Carson within American culture, including one by a puzzled Richard A. Posner, who wondered in his book, *Public Intellectuals,* why Rachel Carson had more citations in [Internet database] LexisNexis than the French Deconstructionist [literary critic] Jacque Derrida. What a perfect metaphor for Rachel Carson's impact. After all, didn't she deconstruct the entire chemical industry until we were able to see, collectively, the essence of what it does—destruction of natural systems—where the dark toxic roots of pesticides were exposed?

And she continues to guide us.

Recently, an open letter was signed and sent to the U.S. Senate to ban reproductive cloning and to place a moratorium on therapeutic cloning by a broad coalition of scientists, environmentalists, feminists, healthcare workers, religious leaders, political leaders, philosophers, and writers. If Rachel Carson were alive, her name would have appeared on that list.

Similar political actions have been taken to elucidate the dangers of genetic engineering, from the possibility of infecting wild salmon populations to the perils of genetically modified foods. Rachel Carson understood that tampering with nature is tampering with health in the broadest, ecological sense. . . .

## Carson and Courage

I want to recall and remember Rachel Carson's spirit. I want to be both fierce and passionate at once. I want to remember that our character has been shaped by the diversity of America's landscape and it is precisely that character that will protect it. I want to carry a sense of indignation inside me to shatter the complacency that has seeped into our society in the name of all we have lost. Call it sacred rage, a rage that is

*Rachel Carson studies wildlife in the woods near her home in Colesville, Maryland, where she wrote* Silent Spring. © Alfred Eisenstaedt/Time & Life Pictures/Getty Images.

grounded in the knowledge that all life is intertwined. I want to know and continue to learn from the grace of wild things that hold a power that sustains hope.

Can we find the moral courage within us to step forward and openly question every law, person, and practice that denies justice toward nature?

Can we continue in this American tradition of bearing witness to beauty and terror which is its own form of advocacy?

And do we have the imagination to rediscover an authentic patriotism that inspires empathy and reflection over pride and naturalism?

Rachel Carson's name is synonymous with courage. She dared to expose the underbelly of the chemical industry and how it was disrupting the balance of nature. In *Silent Spring* we see her signature strength on the page where a confluence of poetry and politics and sound science can create an ethic of place.

But perhaps Rachel Carson's true courage lies in her willingness to align science with the sacred, to admit that her bond toward nature is a spiritual one.

> I am not afraid of being thought a sentimentalist when I say that I believe natural beauty has a necessary place in the spiritual development of any individual or any society. I believe that when ever we destroy beauty, or whatever we substitute something man-made and artificial for a natural feature of the earth, we have retarded some part of man's spiritual growths.

# Social Issues in Literature

# CHAPTER 2

# The Environment in *Silent Spring*

# Silent Spring Advocates a Balanced View of Nature

*Priscilla Coit Murphy*

*Priscilla Coit Murphy is an independent scholar who lives in Chapel Hill, North Carolina.*

*In the following viewpoint, Murphy presents an overview of Silent Spring, tracing the book through its seventeen chapters, pointing out precisely what the book says, and what it does not say. She views Carson's work as a call to action, a warning to humankind of the dangers of imbalance when it comes to the natural world. The idea of taking a balanced view of nature had been around long before Carson wrote her book, Murphy explains, but she points out that it was always seen as an irrationally sentimental attitude. Carson used facts and a well-reasoned approach in order to make her case, Murphy suggests, but asserts that many of her critics have purposefully ignored the logic of her arguments.*

S*ilent Spring* begins with a "Fable for Tomorrow" (which would be parodied by several critics) describing a town "in the heart of America" that had suffered "a strange blight" that killed animals and sickened or even killed families with "mysterious maladies." The result is "a strange stillness. The birds, for example—where had they gone? . . . It was a spring without voices." The only clue was a "white, granular powder" that some weeks earlier had "fallen like snow upon the roofs and the lawns, the fields and streams." In an indirect comparison to radioactive fallout, Carson explains that "no witchcraft, no enemy action had silenced the rebirth of new life in this

Priscilla Coit Murphy, "Chapter 1: *Silent Spring* and Its Contexts: 'The Right to Know,'" *What A Book Can Do: The Publication and Reception of "Silent Spring,"* University of Massachusetts Press, 2005, pp. 5–9. Copyright © 2005 by University of Massachusetts Press. Reproduced by permission.

stricken world. The people had done it themselves." She concludes the chapter saying that the town does not yet exist but that it easily could, and indeed several communities had already suffered one or another form of the disaster. She writes, "What has already silenced the voices of spring in countless towns in America? This book is an attempt to explain."

## The Right to Know

Her second chapter—which would be pivotal in the controversy—defines the problem as Carson saw it, presents her philosophical reasons for writing the book, and makes explicit that she does not argue for a complete ban of pesticides. "We have subjected enormous numbers of people to contact with these poisons, without their consent and often without their knowledge. If the Bill of Rights contains no guarantee that a citizen shall be secure against lethal poisons distributed either by private individuals or by public officials, it is surely only because our forefathers . . . could conceive of no such problem." At the chapter's end, she quotes Rostand: "The obligation to endure gives us the right to know."

The next chapters pursue the proposition that chemical pesticides—agents to control insects, plant diseases, and weeds—present a threat that had been inadequately investigated, for both societal and economic reasons.

> There is still a very limited awareness of the nature of the threat. This is an era of specialists, each of whom sees his own problem and is unaware of or intolerant of the larger frame into which it fits. It is also an era dominated by industry, in which the right to make a dollar at whatever cost is seldom challenged. When the public protests, confronted with some obvious evidence of damaging results of pesticide applications, it is fed little tranquilizing pills of half truth. We urgently need an end to these false assurances, to the sugar coating of unpalatable facts. It is the public that is being asked to assume the risks that the insect controllers calculate.

Pointing out the commonalities of effect and consequence between insecticides and herbicides, she expands the discussion to pesticides in general, making the point that the term "pest" is relative—what is a pestilence in one situation may be a critical need in another.

Her third chapter, "Elixirs of Death," discusses the chemical formulas and properties of the various insecticides, explaining how such chemicals as DDT harm all living organisms in the same way that they harm or kill their intended victims. "Surface Waters and Underground Seas" next describes the continuity of earth's aquatic system of rivers and oceans and how pollution is thereby a potentially uncontainable evil. "It is not possible to add pesticides to water anywhere without threatening the purity of water everywhere." The fifth chapter, "Realms of the Soil," lays out the genesis and life of the soil, dependent as it is on organisms living as well as dead. "Earth's Green Mantle" refers to the "web of life in which there are intimate and essential relations between plants and the earth, between plants and other plants, between plants and animals." In "Needless Havoc," Carson turns to the frequency with which "eradication" campaigns against, for example, the Japanese beetle had been completely unsuccessful after all—causing ecological mayhem but failing to get rid of the targeted problem and even creating in some cases particularly favorable conditions for increasing abundance of the targeted "pest."

## Poisoning Nature

The eighth chapter, "And No Birds Sing," was the inspiration to her editor and publisher, Paul Brooks, for the title of the book. It begins, "Over increasingly large areas of the United States, spring now comes unheralded by the return of the birds, and the early mornings are strangely silent where once they were filled with the beauty of bird song." The next few chapters follow essentially the same format—presenting one aspect of the problem, providing explanations and illustrative incidents, and concluding with exhortations to acknowledge the problem and demand solutions. "Rivers of Death," which focuses on perils and catastrophes among fish life, concludes that the threat to fisheries "by the chemicals entering our waters can no longer be doubted." Carson asks, "When will the public become sufficiently aware of the facts to demand . . . action?"

The next chapter, "Beyond the Dreams of the Borgias," carries some of Carson's most confrontational material, and the title's image would recur in media coverage. The chapter addresses the hazards of aerial spraying against gypsy moths and Japanese beetles as well as crop dusting. In it, Carson challenges the Food and Drug Administration (FDA) on the issue of contamination of consumer foodstuffs, comparing the situation of the public to guests of the Borgias [aristocratic family noted for poisoning their enemies], having no idea what sort of poison might be present in their food. "To the question 'But doesn't the government protect us from such things?' the answer is, 'Only to a limited extent.'"

The next three, somewhat more technical, chapters detail the physiologic and cellular effects, often delayed, of ingestion of pesticides into the human body. "One in Every Four" addresses cancer specifically (noting, among others, studies dealing with the consequences of arsenic used by tobacco growers). "Nature Fights Back" describes processes by which nature adapts to and overcomes threats to survival, including mutations and increased resistance on the part of the "pests" targeted by chemical pesticides. The sixteenth chapter suggests the possibility that resistant strains of insects might eventually overwhelm known methods of control and that epidemics of once-controlled diseases such as malaria could recur with devastating effect. In her concluding chapter, she discusses the scientific possibility of alternative, nonchemical, natural means of pest control.

*A hardcover edition of Rachel Carson's influential work* Silent Spring, *which describes the environmental damage caused by chemical pesticides.* © Victor de Schwanberg/Alamy.

Throughout her discussion, Carson frequently raised questions about why pesticide abuse had not yet been well investigated or discussed, why research into less toxic means of pest control had been limited or ignored, and who was responsible for the failure to protect the general public. Her view of the relationships among industry, government, and research was clear, as was her attitude regarding the economic priorities of the era. Concerning the "otherwise mystifying fact that certain outstanding entomologists are among the leading advocates of chemical control," she explained: "Inquiry into the background of some of these men reveals that their entire research program is supported by the chemical industry. Their professional prestige, sometimes their very jobs depend on the perpetuation of chemical methods. Can we then expect them to bite the hand that literally feeds them?"

## The Balance of Nature

*Silent Spring* is, overall, a call to action based on a carefully delineated explanation of the threat—current and future—of damage to life by misuse of pesticides. "The public must decide whether it wishes to continue on the present road, and it can do so only when in full possession of the facts." The underlying logic of her argument follows from the concept of natural interrelatedness of all living things and the need to sustain those relationships in a dynamic balance. The shorthand for that idea—"the balance of nature"—was a term used before Rachel Carson's era; but until *Silent Spring*, it carried connotations of irrational sentimentality and was applied derisively to the beliefs of conservationists and nature lovers. The legacy of *Silent Spring* was not only to have prompted debate and action on the specific issue of pesticide abuse but also to have made vivid, accessible, and acceptable the idea that nature requires balance, an idea that formed the basis of popularized environmentalism in the coming decades.

Finally, two characteristics of *Silent Spring* must be kept in mind as its career in the public eye is explored. First are the appended fifty-five pages of bibliography and source material, unprecedented in any of Carson's previous works or in any other popular nature books of the time. Prominent in the front matter is an "Author's Note": "I have not wished to burden the text with footnotes but I realize that many of my readers will wish to pursue some of the subjects discussed. I have therefore included a list of my principal sources of information, arranged by chapter and page, in an appendix which will be found at the back of the book." The presence of that reference material was to play a pivotal role in criticism and defense of the book. With respect to the conduct of the debate, even more important is the fact that Carson explicitly declined to prescribe total abstinence from pesticides. Early on, in the second chapter, she makes the following statement (emphasis added): "*It is not my contention that chemical insecticides must never be used.* I do contend that we have put poisonous and biologically potent chemicals indiscriminately into the hands of persons largely or wholly ignorant of their potentials for harm." Many of her critics chose to ignore that disclaimer, however, as well as the proposed alternatives discussed in her final chapter.

# Silent Spring Calls for a New Way of Thinking About the Environment

## John Burnside

*John Burnside is a Scottish poet and novelist. He is the author of more than twenty books, including the poetry collection* The Asylum Dance *and two memoirs,* A Lie About My Father *and* Waking Up in Toytown.

*In the following viewpoint, which appeared in 2002 to commemorate the fortieth anniversary of* Silent Spring's *publication, Burnside contends that the pesticide question raised by Carson's book overshadowed more important concerns. While the debate over the book focused narrowly on the widespread use of DDT, Burnside explains, Carson was urging humanity to think more deeply about its relationship with the environment, to shed the emphasis on the notion of controlling nature for a new philosophy of living in harmony with nature by understanding that humans are a part of the natural world rather than the supreme masters of the environment. Burnside argues that humans have failed to learn the lessons that Carson taught: her teachings were not the hysterical ravings of a woman out on the edge, but sensible suggestions challenging people to alter the way they view the world.*

In 1962, a powerful group of chemical industry representatives, government officials and salaried "experts" on the environment set out to prevent the publication of a much-loved naturalist's last book. The naturalist in question was Rachel Carson, bestselling author of books about the sea; the last book was Silent Spring. It is a moment every life-respecting

John Burnside, "Saturday Review: Reluctant Crusader," *Guardian* (London, England), May 18, 2002, p. 1. Reproduced by permission of the author.

person cherishes: like the lone protester in Tiananmen Square [who stood in front of approaching Chinese military tanks and symbolized the forcible removal of protestors from the square on June 5, 1989], halting a column of tanks with nothing more than his hopelessly vulnerable body, Carson placed herself—her reputation, her failing health—in the path of the juggernaut that, at the time, everyone still blithely referred to as "progress"—and slowed it a little.

## A New Way of Thinking

The narrowest of the book's objectives—a review of the aerial spraying of DDT over American towns, farmland and forests—was achieved, and government policy on pesticides was significantly altered. Its wider objective—to radicalise our thinking about our relationship with the natural world—was barely recognised. At the same time, the storm of controversy and argument it provoked set the tone of our environmental debates for much of the 40 years since its publication: debates that rarely address the most fundamental principles of Carson's thinking.

For Carson, as much as for [German philosopher Martin] Heidegger, say, what the 20th century demanded was a new way of thinking about the world. She demanded, not just an end to indiscriminate pesticide use, but a new science, a new philosophy. "The 'control of nature' is a phrase conceived in arrogance," she said, at the conclusion of *Silent Spring*, "born of the Neanderthal age of biology and philosophy, when it was supposed that nature exists for the convenience of man."

This new way of thinking might now be characterised as "deep" or "radical" ecology. Since *Silent Spring*, a great deal of effort has gone into its suppression. As [Professor] Jonathan Bate has pointed out, the two other radical movements that emerged in the 1960s, feminism and anti-racism, have been tolerated: gender and postcolonial studies are offered in most universities, for example. Radical ecology, a philosophy that challenges all the accepted social and economic models, lags far behind.

This is because it is a genuine threat, not just to vested interests within the structure, but to the structure itself, for it asks us to dismantle our most basic assumptions: about how we do business, about how we use natural "resources," about how we live. In 1962, *Silent Spring* made that threat real in a way that took both government and big business by surprise— and they have been trying to avoid being caught out again ever since.

## Responding to a Need

Carson did not want to write *Silent Spring*. True, she was painfully aware of the indiscriminate use of pesticides, and had proposed articles on the problem to the magazines she was writing for as far back as the late 1940s, but *Silent Spring* was, in many ways, not her kind of project. In her great sea trilogy, *Under The Sea Wind* (1941), *The Sea Around Us* (1951) and *The Edge Of The Sea* (1956), a singular voice emerges, at once rigorous and lyrical, a voice she had come to know as her own. It was not, in so many ways, the right voice for a "crusading" book on DDT. By 1957, however, the pesticide problem was totally out of hand, as an attempt to prevent "an infestation of gypsy moths" in the city of New York clearly demonstrated: "The gypsy moth," Carson wrote, "is a forest insect, certainly not an inhabitant of cities. Nor does it live in meadows, cultivated fields, gardens or marshes. Nevertheless, the planes hired by the United States Department of Agriculture and the New York Department of Agriculture and Markets showered down the prescribed DDT-in-fuel-oil with impartiality. They sprayed truck gardens and dairy farms, fish ponds and salt marshes. They sprayed the quarter-acre lots of suburbia, drenching a housewife making a desperate effort to cover her garden before the roaring plane reached her, and showering insecticide over children at play and commuters at railway stations. At Setauket [Long Island] a fine quarter horse drank from a trough in a field which the planes had sprayed: 10 hours later it was dead."

This was probably the single event that most influenced Carson to embark properly on *Silent Spring*. She had hoped to find a more appropriate person to take the book on: an investigative journalist, ideally, who could weave together all the diverse strands of anecdotal and scientific evidence, political background and shady manoeuvring. But when nobody emerged, she set to work, knowing that it would cost her far too much, in time and effort. "There would be no peace for me," she said, "if I kept silent."

Though it exposed the scandal of pesticide abuse to a stunned world, *Silent Spring* was the last book Carson wrote. She died of cancer in 1964. Ironically, the other project she had been contemplating, one more suited to her temperament, concerned the weather.

"For months (or perhaps years) before I suddenly felt called upon to write about insecticides," she wrote to Paul Brooks, author of *The Pursuit Of Wilderness*, "I have been considering the problem of what living things do to change or even control their environment. It has many aspects (including the vital one of weather control) and this pollution of soil and vegetation is only one of them." One wonders what impact such a project might have had on the science of global warming.

## A Towering Achievement

*Silent Spring* was serialised in the *New Yorker*, beginning June 16 1962, and published complete on September 27. It would be a mistake to see it simply as a book about pesticides, though that was how it was quickly characterised by its opponents, who wanted to portray Carson as anti-chemicals and hence anti-progress.

In fact, some of Carson's best writing goes into the book, as she carries her readers along with the argument. Most of all, she wanted people to see the background to the problem of DDT, as in this passage where she discusses agriculture and business: "We are told that the enormous and expanding use of pesticides is necessary to maintain farm production. Yet is our real problem not one of over-production? Our farms, despite measures to remove acreages from production and to pay farmers not to produce, have yielded such a staggering excess of crops that the American taxpayer in 1962 is paying out more than $1bn [billion] a year as the total carrying cost of the surplus food storage programme. And is the situation helped when one branch of the agriculture department tries to reduce production while another states, as it did in 1958, 'It is believed generally that a reduction of crop acreages under provisions of the soil bank will stimulate interest in use of chemicals to obtain maximum production on the land retained in crops.'"

As the book progresses, Carson is a careful guide through the complex web of political and fiscal shenanigans, explaining to a public that would have known almost nothing about biological, as opposed to chemical, pest control exactly how government and other bodies manipulated the figures to make the biological option always seem "too expensive."

In this alone, *Silent Spring* is a towering achievement: Carson makes the necessary case against DDT, but on the way, she exposes the entire system. As Paul Brooks notes, in his excellent study of her work, *The House Of Life*, "she was questioning not only the indiscriminate use of poisons but the basic irresponsibility of an industrialised, technological society toward the natural world."

## Confronting Her Critics

The response from that society was not long in coming. Soon the men in grey were creeping out from behind their retorts and balance sheets, ready to attack. *The New Yorker* serialisation had taken everyone by surprise; now, every effort was made to suppress or vilify the book, not only by chemical companies such as Velsicol and Monsanto, and the National Agricultural Chemicals Association, but also by government departments, the Nutrition Foundation, and even baby food producers.

It made no difference. Carson was well prepared for the attacks; not only would she not be intimidated, she even refused to go out of her way to defend her position, saying the book could look after itself. When she did feel the need to strike back, however, she was characteristically effective: one reviewer, she said, "was offended because I made the statement that it is customary for pesticide manufacturers to support research on chemicals in the universities . . . I can scarcely believe the reviewer is unaware of it, because his own university is among those receiving such grants."

She went on: "Such a liaison between science and industry is a growing phenomenon, seen in other areas as well. The American Medical Association, through its newspaper, has just referred physicians to a pesticide trade association for information to help them answer patients' questions about the effects of pesticides on man.

"I am sure physicians have a need for information on this subject. But I would like to see them referred to authoritative scientific or medical literature—not to a trade organisation whose business it is to promote the sale of pesticides." She concluded: "When the scientific organisation speaks, whose voice do we hear—that of science? Or of the sustaining industry?"

Meanwhile, the public, and most of the popular press, loved *Silent Spring*. It became a best-seller, a talking point in factories and drawing rooms, the subject of hundreds of newspaper articles, parodies, cartoons and debates. More importantly, it reached the office of [President] John F. Kennedy, who asked his scientific adviser, Jerome B. Wiesner, to begin a study of the whole DDT question. A pesticides committee was set up, and quickly produced a report criticising the chemical companies and endorsing Carson's views. Something had been achieved.

But only a little. Testifying to that same committee in June 1963, Carson took the opportunity to remind the world of the wider implications of her work: "We still talk in terms of conquest. We still haven't become mature enough to think of ourselves as only a tiny part of a vast and incredible universe. Man's attitude toward nature is today critically important simply because we have now acquired a fateful power to alter and destroy nature. But man is part of nature and his war against nature is inevitably a war against himself."

## Forty Years Later

[In 2002] it is 40 years since that statement. During that time, the nature of pesticide development, presentation and especially marketing, has changed a good deal. The chemical companies learned much from their first skirmish with a determined and well-respected campaigner. In fact, corporations have become highly skilled in managing public opinion—and one of their first steps was to consolidate the "support" for institutions of learning that Carson so astutely noted.

In 1962, the field where battles were fought, in public at least, was scientific debate; the trick then was to have control over the nature, terms and extent of the debate. An unexpected bonus, in recent years, has come from public awareness of that control; now, when the scientific organisation speaks, the voice we hear is too often that of the sustaining industry, as the MMR scandal so clearly demonstrates. We do not know who to trust, and in such cases, we tend to hope that our leaders and elected representatives are still as well meaning as they seemed when we voted for them.

Meanwhile, spring has become a little more silent, and all the seasons considerably noisier, with each passing year. A recent study concluded that the number of sparrows in Edinburgh's Princes Street Gardens [in Scotland] was falling because the birds were unable to hear their own songs through the thunder of traffic that roars through the city every day, hour after miserable hour.

With their songs of courtship and territory disappearing, it is not simply that the birds can no longer breed; they are no longer meaningfully there at all. They live in an Eraserhead world [after the film by David Lynch] of background noise, haunted by the odd plaintive, half-heard whisper of fellowship. Meanwhile, the skylarks and warblers that used to be so plentiful in our countryside are vanishing, especially on those big, "profitable" farms the government seems to favour, because, as Adam Harrison of WWF [World Wide Fund for Nature] Scotland says, "The public pays for a farming policy that pollutes, then pays to clear up that pollution and pays yet again at the supermarket for the food we buy." In Scotland the only reason we have "clean" water is because the European Commission threatens to take legal action against our executive if it does not establish appropriate measures to prevent wholesale pollution of streams with nitrate fertilisers by those same subsidised farmers.

## A Radical Philosophy of Life

Part of the reason for this lamentable situation is that business and government have mostly succeeded in keeping us all in two minds about ecology as a workable philosophy for daily life. The most calculated criticisms of Carson made in the wake of *Silent Spring* were that she was mystical or sentimental—and somehow that view of philosophical ecology has stuck.

Yet mystical and sentimental is exactly what ecology is not: these honours belong to the old religions of market values and objectivity. If Carson were alive today, she would be em-phasising our need to understand how central the philosophy of ecology is to our lives. What she wanted to show us was not that everything was interconnected, as in some web or lat-tice—to use the current, popular cybernetics model—but that matter is continuous, like a Celtic knot. This continuum, she believed, was the one single narrative that includes all others.

In its attack on *Silent Spring, Time* [magazine] described her case as "unfair, one-sided and hysterically over-emphatic. Many of the scary generalisations . . . are patently unsound. 'It is not possible,' says Miss Carson, 'to add pesticides to water anywhere without threatening the purity of water everywhere.' It takes only a moment of reflection to show that this is non-sense."

But this is exactly the point: you cannot pollute water lo-cally. All waters come together, as all life does: "Individual ele-ments are lost to view, only to reappear again and again in different incarnations in a kind of material immortality. Kin-dred forces to those which, in some period inconceivably re-mote, gave birth to that primal bit of protoplasm tossing on the ancient seas continue their mighty and incomprehensible work. Against this cosmic background the life span of a par-ticular plant or animal appears, not as a drama complete in it-self, but only as a brief interlude in a panorama of endless change."

This is not mystical; it is certainly far from hysteria. It is a call to a new way of thinking, a challenge to us all, to create, and live by, a radical philosophy of life.

# Silent Spring's Success Stems from Its Mix of Science and Storytelling

*Dianne Newell*

*Dianne Newell teaches in the Department of History at the University of British Columbia. She is the author of numerous books and articles on Canadian history and science fiction.*

*In the following viewpoint, Newell stresses an aspect of* Silent Spring *that she argues is often overlooked due to its sensational content: the writing itself. Carson always wanted to be an author, Newell explains, and her storytelling ability drives* Silent Spring. *Carson was a bold, thoughtful, inventive writer, Newell states, and she draws on techniques from fiction and, particularly, science fiction and apocalyptic tales, to depict a perilous future if the spraying of toxic pesticides is allowed to continue unchecked. Carson is a science storyteller, Newell concludes, whose powerful tale hooked readers.*

Rachel Carson ... was likely not a fan of science fiction, and did not live to see feminist critiques of science. Yet, she recognized the persuasive power of the science fiction form in telling an apocalyptic story about science.... [S]he was a daring, experimental writer of the postwar era, and her influence over the public debate about science and society has been international in scope and enduring. [S]he ... endeavored from the margins to find the social meaning in science.

## The Importance of Storytelling

Carson always promoted the importance of a storytelling quality in nature writing. She once even claimed that in college her ambition to be a writer barely lost out to her passion

Dianne Newell, "Judith Merril and Rachel Carson: Reflections on Their 'Potent Fictions' of Science," *Journal of International Women's Studies*, vol. 5, no. 4, 2004, p. 31. Reproduced by permission.

for natural history. She was also proud of the literary content of her science writings. She always credited the literary merit of her work for her ability to reach a large, popular audience of non-specialists with her science stories of the natural world. She was already an innovative, national best-selling author in the natural sciences well before the appearance of *Silent Spring*. By the early 1950s, she had won major awards and honorary doctorates in both literature and science, and membership in the American Academy of Arts and Letters, which was unusual for a woman, let alone a scientist. Hers was a remarkable, pre-feminist success in lowering the barriers, not just between women and science, but likewise between science and literature.

Carson's attention to literary matters, to poetics and emotion, to fostering a sense of wonder in her science writing represented a political choice, political in the sense of challenging established ideas about her field. Ceremonies for Carson's prestigious book award and the political and policy upheavals in her own government service in the early 1950s provided her with opportunities to speak her mind as an advocate for the natural world and—much as Merril had—to speculate about possible futures. Carson's recent biographer, Linda Lear, notes that Carson used the occasion of accepting the National Book Award for Nonfiction in 1952 to comment on her concern with the trend toward the 'artificial separation of science and literature as exclusive methods of investigating the world.' For Carson, 'the aim of science is to discover and illuminate the truth,' which was for her the objective of all literature. Carson's conclusion that 'there can be no separate literature of science' was both unusual for the times and a harbinger for the feminist debates about science to come.

Carson continued the theme when accepting the John Burroughs Medal [named for the famous nature writer] for excellence in nature writing the same year. On that occasion she argued that natural science writing as public education was an urgent need if Americans were to prevent the type of human isolation in increasingly artificial, 'man-made' worlds, isolation that fostered what she chillingly described as 'experiments for the destruction of himself and his world.' She underscored her message about the social obligation of nature writing in the atomic age: 'If we have ever regarded our interest in natural history as an escape from the realities of our modern world, let us now reverse this attitude. For the mysteries of living things, and the birth and death of continents and seas, are among its great realities.'

## Making a Difference

Carson's anti-pesticide study, *Silent Spring*, reflects the hand of the same thoughtful, inventive writer and visionary. It also demonstrates her continuing resistance to the idea of a separate literature of science. Nevertheless, it is much bolder and experimental than her earlier writings. Lear argues that its polemical [argumentative] nature was a major departure from Carson's earlier writing, because in it Carson [. . .] attacked the integrity of the scientific establishment, its moral leadership, and its direction of society. She exposed their self-interest as well as their poor science and defended the public's right to know the truth. Carson had wanted the book to make a difference, and, as is well known, it did. *Silent Spring* launched the modern environmental movement, has been compared with [English naturalist] Charles Darwin's *On the Origin of Species* for the scope of its challenge to the dominant scientific paradigm, and it remains one of the most important American books of the twentieth century.

Carson arrived at this departure from her usual nature writing by grounding her radical analysis of the dangers posed by the indiscriminate use of synthetic pesticides in a difficult maze of obscure scientific studies and investigative journalism. Her wartime role as an 'information specialist' and a government editor and writer of fish and wildlife research publications had already exposed her to early classified government science on the dangers to wildlife and human health of the DDT pesticide range. Her former editorial role in government, which might seem on the surface to have been an inferior position, given her training as a marine biologist, proved a tremendous asset after she left government service in the early 1950s for a career as an independent scholar-writer. It gave her the access to the classified core research and to the researchers she needed for her controversial new study that her free-lance position might have prevented.

## A Female Support System

The writing of *Silent Spring* from 1957 to its publication in 1962 would also draw Carson into a dynamic shifting network of concerned, tenacious, and unusually influential women on the margins of science in the United States, Canada, and Britain. These women both prompted and advocated Carson's study. The book project was thus Carson's entree into an expanding world of women activists in North America and Europe, though she would die of breast cancer in 1964 before she had a chance to enter fully into that powerful arena. Several of these women are identified by Linda Lear in her writings on Carson, as well as by Carson herself. She writes in *Silent Spring* of the influential appeals of her friend Olga Huckins, whose private bird sanctuary was poisoned by pesticides in the 1950s in an aerial spraying campaign for mosquito control. The early stages of Carson's research for the book and the articles and letters she published at the time drew the attention of Washington Post newspaper owner Agnes Meyer, and activist Christine Stevens, who was president of the Animal Welfare Institute of New York. Stevens recognized the value of Carson's special qualities as a nature writer for environmental causes, writing to Carson: 'All humanitarians will be grateful to you for writing on this subject, for your great gift as a writer combined with those of a biologist would make your efforts of inestimable value in putting a stop to these poison campaigns.' She introduced Carson to the work of British environmental activist Ruth Harrison, whose expose of the inhuman treatment of livestock when published in 1963 would carry a preface written by Carson.

## Using Science Fiction Conventions

Carson constructed this extraordinary book in the second wave of nuclear awareness and concern, which [historian Paul] Boyer suggests now "surfaced at all cultural levels." Examining the impact of the bomb on Carson's anti-pesticide narratives, [author] Ralph Lutts concludes that Carson most certainly counted on that public awareness and fear of radioactive contamination in constructing the story line of the book. Carson used the popular narratives of the day (fear of nuclear war and radiation sickness, invisible killers, hidden persuaders), drawing parallels between the effects of atomic radiation and those of chemical pesticides, and the persuasive power of mass advertising. All of them were major topics in mass-marketed science fiction, thanks to the radical Cold War science fiction writers such as Judith Merril.

Finally, in her attention to the literary quality of her science writing, Carson also employed science/speculative fiction-like conventions and ideas that were 'in the air'—although there is no evidence to support the idea that she did so intentionally. On the contrary, fragmentary evidence exists to suggest that Carson was not familiar with science fiction literature and not even interested in getting to know it. Yet, like her postwar contemporaries in science fiction, she would have understood the appeal of images of the 'near future.' In science fiction practice, the near future setting is a world 'imminently real' (it could be tomorrow), in which people may someday live and must imaginatively prepare for in advance. Taken as a whole, Carson's literary choices were unorthodox for a natural science writer. They were also courageous choices. Some crit-

*An agricultural town in California is fogged with the chemical pesticide DDT in the early 1950s.* © Loomis Dean/Time & Life Pictures/Getty Images.

ics of the day disparaged *Silent Spring* as an entire work of science fiction (referring to the low regard in which science fiction was held, possibly even by Carson).

Many of them scoffed at Carson's myth-like reputation as a goddess of nature (referring to the environmental and animal rights activists with whom she associated), called her emotional and extremist, questioned her integrity, sanity, and loyalty to the nation, even branded the 55-year old Carson a 'spinster,' the ultimate heavy-handed insult leveled against women who stepped [out] of bounds.

## A Science Storyteller

No aspect of *Silent Spring* is more 'potent' than the prologue. Carson chose to write it as a fable, 'A Fable for Tomorrow.' The growing scholarship exploring the public response to *Silent Spring* is mindful of the contemporary appeal of Carson's apocalyptic vision and of the special role of the fable prologue in cementing that vision. The near-future images in Carson's fable prologue are meant to appeal to a reader's creative imagination to end the destructive impulse that marked the reality of the postwar era, a reality about which she had been issuing gentle public warnings since at least 1952. The narrator of the book's science-fable prologue imagines a silent springtime in a world destroyed by its own citizens through the indiscriminate use of pesticides. Reverting to her own authorial voice in a final paragraph, Carson confides in readers that it is not too late for America to prevent the story in the fable. However, she wrote, 'a grim specter has crept upon us almost unnoticed, and this imagined tragedy [described in the fable] may easily become a stark reality we all shall know. What has already silenced the voices of spring in countless towns in America?' The answer to Carson's powerful science-fiction-like question is the subject of the entire book. The reader is hooked. What a science storyteller, in [American author Donna] Haraway's positive sense of the term. And what a science story.

# Silent Spring Is a Subversive Book

## Gary Kroll

*Gary Kroll is associate professor of history at the State University of New York at Plattsburgh, where he teaches courses in the history of ecology and environmentalism. He is the author of* America's Ocean Wilderness: A Cultural History of Twentieth-Century Exploration.

*In the following viewpoint, Kroll contends that* Silent Spring *is a subversive text that quietly goes about trying to change the way humans interact with nature. The book is about much more than simply curtailing pesticide use, he asserts, but most people misinterpreted it in this way. According to Kroll, rather than viewing humans as arrogant masters of the natural environment, the book advocates that people seek to reframe their lives in harmony with the natural world. This message never took hold, Kroll suggests, because the mainstream environmental movement of the 1970s that Carson ushered in was co-opted by commercial capitalism. But Kroll maintains that Carson's message lives on in contemporary grassroots attempts to bring humans into equanimity with nature. He concludes that such activism is a long overdue realization of the true nature of ecological thinking in which Carson believed.*

In the late 1960s Paul Shepard, a human ecologist and philosopher, wrote the introduction for *Subversive Science*—a book that offered an interdisciplinary perspective on what was then termed "the ecological crisis." Shepard noted that a change in western perspective was absolutely necessary: "where

Gary Kroll, "Rachel Carson—*Silent Spring*: A Brief History of Ecology as a Subversive Subject." Reprinted from *Reflections*, vol. 9, no. 2, 2002, with permission of the Program for Ethics, Science, and the Environment, Department of Philosophy, Oregon State University.

now there is man-centeredness, even pathology of isolation and fear. . .ecology as applied to man faces the task of renewing a balanced view." Ecology was less important as a scientific discipline than for its holistic perspective. There is, Shepard maintained, much that is radical in ecology: "The ideological status of ecology is that of a resistance movement. Its Rachel Carsons and [ecologist] Aldo Leopolds are subversive (as [ecologist Paul] Sears recently called ecology itself)." He concluded by noting that the ecological crisis could not be ameliorated by technical and scientifically engineered quick-fixes, but rather by invoking "an element of humility which is foreign to our thought, which moves us to silent wonder and glad affirmation." While the point is debatable, one could certainly argue that Shepard's, Leopold's, and Carson's revolution never took place, at least not in the manner that they had hoped.

## *Silent Spring* as a Subversive Book

Rachel Carson's *Silent Spring* played a large role in articulating ecology as a "subversive subject"—as a perspective that cut against the grain of materialism, scientism, and the technologically engineered control of nature. But ecology's subversive moment proved all too brief, and by the first Earth Day in 1970, American environmentalism was headed in a very different direction. I want to examine briefly the subversive nature of ecology in the 1960s and demonstrate Carson's participation in that dialog; I also want to offer a few explanations for why this subversive vision never materialized. But if a subversively ecological perspective was not the legacy of *Silent Spring*, then what was? My claim is that an important legacy of *Silent Spring* is the adoption of a very healthy and widespread skepticism concerning the scientific control of both the body and the environment.

*Silent Spring* laid bare a curious split within science that had its origin in the disputes between naturalists and experimental biologists of the early twentieth century. On the one hand, Carson speaks with the authoritative voice of ecology—a rational discipline by the 1960s wholly accepted by the scientific community at large for its rigorous and falsifiable methods of interpreting nature. On the other hand, Carson speaks as the critic of science; she did this in two ways. First, she takes aim at the overly mechanical and reductive sciences—economic entomology [the scientific study of insects] and organic chemistry in this instance—that isolate nature to the neglect of interconnections. Secondly, she critiques the wider—and perhaps more nebulous—cultural authority of science and technology to control nature. The two come together in the often-quoted final paragraph of Silent Spring.

> The "control of nature" is a phrase conceived in arrogance, born of the Neanderthal age of biology and philosophy, when it was supposed that nature exists for the convenience of man. . . . It is our alarming misfortune that so primitive a science has armed itself with the most modern and terrible weapons, and that in turning them against the insects it has also turned them against the earth.

The point was more graphically presented in the CBS News Reports documentary, "Rachel Carson's *Silent Spring*." The program created a clear dichotomy between laboratory science—accompanied by shots of factories and dams—and the "softer" side of Carson's ecology that had a strange ability to speak as a science while at the same time appearing very other than the stereotype of science. Many of my students, for example, are surprised to hear that Carson had a graduate degree from one of the premier universities for experimental biology.

It was precisely this ambiguity that Shepard and Sears were articulating when they called ecology a "subversive subject." Radical ecology emerged from the disciplinary matrix of academic ecology. The Leopold of *Sand County Almanac* [his collection of essays on environmental ethics] emerged from the Leopold of the U.S. Forest Service. Similarly, Carson's subversive ecology emerged from the laboratories of Johns Hopkins University and the offices of the U.S. Fish and Wildlife Service. The voices of Carson, Sears and Leopold merged with other critical currents in the postwar era. In 1958 a concern over the dangers of nuclear test fallout led [biologist] Barry Commoner and others to organize the St. Louis Committee for Nuclear Information. Echoing Carson's critique, Commoner noted that the Committee emphasized "the balancing of social judgment against cost," decisions that "should be made by every citizen and not left to the experts." Murray Bookchin criticized the uses of pesticides and preservatives in his treatise on human ecology, *Our Synthetic Environment* (1962). Like Carson, he noted that "neither science nor technology, however, is a substitute for a balanced relationship between man and nature." Though the laws that define that relationship are the laws of ecology. Other subversives, like [American writer and intellectual] Paul Goodman, took aim at the entire complex of the scientific-industrial-technocratic and consumer-oriented west. [German philosopher] Herbert Marcuse added fuel to the New Left fire by claiming that "authentic ecology flows into a militant struggle for a socialist politics which must attack the system at its roots, both in the process of production and in the mutilated consciousness of individuals." While Carson rarely waxed on reforming the entirety of western society, there is an element of critical theory in *Silent Spring* that begins to contemplate a wholly new relationship between humans and nature.

## The Rise of Popular Environmentalism

This message was lost to popular environmentalism of the 1970s. The cultural history of *Silent Spring* as an appropriated text has yet to be written. But one can start by looking at [author] Peter Matthiessen's brief *Time* biography for an index to the co-opted *Silent Spring*. Matthiessen makes no reference to

*A student in a gas mask demonstrates in New York City on the first Earth Day, April 22, 1970. Gary Koll argues that mainstream environmentalism, which emerged in the early 1970s, was co-opted by conservative corporate and political forces and does not accurately reflect the values of Rachel Carson or other environmental leaders. © AP Images.*

Carson's calls for humility; he says nothing about the fundamental choices that humans would have to make; *Silent Spring*'s "Other Road"; there is no mention of the ecological interconnectedness of the world that made the threat of toxins so dire. Carson's key contribution, in Matthiessen's estimation, lie in blowing a whistle on the pesticide industry. "True, the damage being done by poison chemicals today is far worse than it was when she wrote the book," Matthiessen tells us. "Yet one shudders to imagine how much more impoverished our habitat would be had *Silent Spring* not sounded the alarm." Carson would have shuddered. *Silent Spring* was so much more than an anti-pesticide tract. It was an essay of ecological radicalism that attempted to wake up a populace quiescent to the techno-scientific control of the world.

This "radical ecology," as [ecofeminist] Carolyn Merchant calls it, quickly flagged in the early 1970s. Indeed, Marcuse's essay on "Ecology and Revolution" noted that the ecology movement had been co-opted by commercial capitalism. For example, a Schlitz malt liquor advertisement appeared in the *New York Times* on the first Earth Day; it shows a man and a woman, hand in hand, strolling along a beautiful and deserted shoreline. Below the photograph is the copy that a Schlitz advertising team carefully constructed to fend off Earth Day criticism. "You've found a beautiful spot? Take us along. We were made for each other. Leaving? Take us along. Drop us off. The nearest trash can'll do. A thing of beauty is a joy forever. We'd like to help keep it that way." Earth Day itself seems to have been artfully orchestrated as a centrist issue by Wisconsin senator Gaylord Nelson and Harvard law student Denis Hayes. As environmentalism became a matter of political consensus dominated by professional environmentalists, ecology lost its subversive edge. Environmental science departments mushroomed in academia over night and embraced the mantra of ecology-but instead of Marcuse, Commoner, Leopold and Carson's subversive and radical ecology, such programs were largely developed with an emphasis on the trophic-dynamic systems of engineered environments. Academic ecology most certainly became one of the conceptual cornerstones of mainstream environmentalism. But it was not a subversive ecology that questioned fundamental values of economics, consumer habits, and techno-scientific control. It represented an engineering mentality in which problems of waste, pollution, population, biodiversity and the toxic environment could be solved scientifically.

## Carson's Legacy Extends Far Beyond Pesticide Control

So if the ecological revolution never materialized in the way that Carson had hoped, what was her legacy to the history of science and society? Over the past thirty years green philosophies like eco-feminism, social ecology, and deep ecology have illustrated increasingly sophisticated systems of thought that attempt to reconfigure the relationships between humans, environment, and the role of science and technology in mediating the human-nature dialectic. The growth of sociology and ethics programs that scrutinize science, technology, and society is especially impressive. While it is doubtful that scientific authorities ever had free reign to do whatever they wished, today they are held to a high degree of accountability. The press actively keeps the public wary with news of genetically engineered organisms, terminator seed manipulations, irradiated food, and new pesticides. While we might question the efficacy of such initiatives in creating real and widespread changes in values, we have come a long way in questioning the epistemic sovereignty of science. Carson was not the first to do this; but she was among the first to bring the debate into the public sphere.

Paralleling these initiatives among America's empowered classes has been the remarkable growth of the environmental justice movement. Since the 1970s, people of color—often living at or below the poverty level—have come together at the grass roots level to mount campaigns against the environmentally racist policies of American industrialism. These points of resistance often arise from degraded urban spaces whose inhabitants have felt particularly victimized by the nonarbitrary placement of incinerators and pollution-producing factories. They have marshaled scientific evidence—often under incredible duress—to oppose these policies of indiscriminate environmental racism. For instance, the "Principles of Environmental Justice" written at the First National People of Color Environmental Leadership Summit in 1991 declares the rights of people of color to develop social, political, cultural, and economic communities—collaborative groups that define their own ecology of existence in opposition to the technocratic top-down directives of modern business, government, and—most notably—the professionalized environmental lobby. In one sense, the environmental justice movement has moved beyond Carson's own vision for a democratically based subversive ecology. Seen from another perspective, it was precisely these social movements that Carson envisioned, and it would be easier for us to recognize the fact if *Silent Spring* was not part of the conservative co-option of the 1970s.

The hope for a resurrected subversive ecology that incorporates a vision of both human and natural diversity seems to be on the rise. But the United States is sitting in the backseat—with some notable exceptions—as world leaders, scientists, and social advocates hash out a new vision of sustaining human existence within nature. This year's World Summit in Johannesburg [South Africa] boasts a truly visionary program in which the environmental sciences will partner up with social and economic justice advocates. Leaders are coming to realize that there will be no technological quick-fix for the global environmental crisis. Global warming is now being conceived of as less a scientific and technological problem than a social and cultural problem, and it is the perspective of ecology, to invoke Shepard again, that lies at the core of this [issue]. Whether or not there is a direct link between *Silent Spring* and the World Summit is besides the point; the Summit promises to be a full realization of Carson's desire to humble humanity into a relationship of equanimity with nature—an overdue actualization of ecology's subversive potential.

# Carson Used War Metaphors to Make Her Point About Pesticides

*Cheryll Glotfelty*

*Cheryll Glotfelty is associate professor of literature and environment at the University of Nevada, Reno. She is coeditor of* The Ecocriticism Reader *and editor of* Literary Nevada: Writings from the Silver State.

*In the following viewpoint, Glotfelty contends that in 1962, with the Cold War between the United States and the Soviet Union serving as a backdrop, Rachel Carson's book struck a chord with Americans in part because she harnessed a familiar metaphor for the conflict between pesticide sprayers and nature. Carson, Glotfelty explains, characterized what an arrogant humanity was doing to the natural world as a war against nature, with the innocent and unknowing American public cast as victims of this battle. To this day, Glotfelty notes, environmentalists continue to use the rhetoric of warfare in their clash with antienvironmentalists, and this rhetoric serves to escalate tensions between the two camps. Though Carson's heightened rhetoric may have been necessary in her day, Glotfelty suggests that it may be time for those who are committed to saving the Earth to rein in the language of conflict.*

**1962**: Rachel Carson's *Silent Spring* is published. The Cuban missile crisis marks the height of U.S.-Soviet tensions, bringing the world to the brink of nuclear war.

Cheryll Glotfelty, "Cold War, Silent Spring: The Trope of War in Modern Environmentalism," *And No Birds Sing: Rhetorical Analyses of Rachel Carson's "Silent Spring,"* edited by Craig Waddell. Carbondale and Edwardsville: Southern Illinois University Press, pp. 158–168. Copyright © 2000 by the Board of Trustees, Southern Illinois University. Reproduced by permission.

In 1962, after *Silent Spring* was serialized, one reader wrote to the *New Yorker*,

> Miss Rachel Carson's reference to the selfishness of insecti-
> cide manufacturers probably reflects her Communist sym-
> pathies, like a lot of our writers these days.
>
> We can live without birds and animals, but, as the current
> market slump shows, we cannot live without business.
>
> As for insects, isn't it just like a woman to be scared to
> death of a few little bugs! As long as we have the H-bomb
> everything will be O.K.

## Cold War Rhetoric and *Silent Spring*

... [T]he genesis, the writing, and even the reception of Rachel Carson's most influential book exactly coincided with the Cold War years in America and were colored by them. Indeed, the very subject of her book—DDT and other synthetic pesticides—was itself a product of war. DDT was first used on a large scale in the Naples typhus epidemic of 1943–44 and continued to be used during the rest of World War II to protect millions of soldiers and civilians against insect-borne diseases. Thanks to DDT, World War II is thought to be the first major war in which more people died from enemy action than from disease. DDT, the miracle chemical of World War II, came to the United States for civilian use in 1945 in a wave of publicity and high hopes. Some called it the atomic bomb of insecticides, the harbinger of a new age in insect control. DDT and its fellow chemicals were heroes, fruits of a new age of science and technology that promised to make life more safe, comfortable, and convenient than ever before.

Causing a remarkable about-face in public opinion, the rhetoric of *Silent Spring* persuaded the public that these miracle pesticides were, in fact, deadly poisons, harmful to *all* living things, just as earlier Cold War rhetoric had convinced the American public that their World War II ally, the Soviet

Union, had become their new worst enemy. After President
Harry Truman delivered the speech that introduced what
would become known as the Truman Doctrine, urging that
the United States assist the democratic nations of Europe in
their struggle against the powerful forces of totalitarianism,
one commentator noted, "We went to sleep in one world and
woke up . . . in another."

*Silent Spring* had a similarly alarming effect upon public
consciousness. It is featured in Robert Downs's *Books That
Changed America* as the book that launched the modern environmental movement. Scholars of American environmental
rhetoric M. Jimmie Killingsworth and Jacqueline S. Palmer assert that "Carson's book established rhetorical conventions
that would become standard fare in the environmentalist debate." *Silent Spring*'s critique of the widespread use of what
were regarded as wonder chemicals was nothing less than an
indictment of modern life itself. Carson's editor and biographer Paul Brooks remarks, "*Silent Spring* has been recognized
throughout the world as one of those rare books that change
the course of history—not through incitement to war or violent revolution, but by altering the direction of man's thinking."

## A New Kind of War

I agree with Brooks that Carson altered the direction of our
thinking, but I argue that *Silent Spring* did instigate a new
kind of war by redirecting the language and concepts of the
Cold War to apply to "man's war against nature." While pesticide manufacturers were waging their all-out war on insects,
Carson started a new "war" against the manufacturers and
pesticide sprayers. They became the new worst enemy. Industry as the enemy has by now become an entrenched way of
thinking in the environmental movement, and the lexicon of
war continues to pervade environmentalist discourse. In this
essay, I examine the way that Carson employs Cold War rhetoric in her effort to mobilize support for a protracted war on
despoilers of the environment.

Pesticide advertisements themselves cleverly exploited Cold War icons. Some pesticide commercials bore a striking resemblance to anti-Communist propaganda, depicting an insect army marching across a map of the United States. The situation looks terribly grim *until* a spray can appears from the sky to kill the hostile invaders dead in their tracks and keep the world safe for democracy, "sprout-less potato[es]," and "mosquitoless patio[s]." Such advertisements equated pest control with national defense and made the spray can a symbol of patriotism.

Given the militant cast of pesticide advertisements, coupled with her own sympathies for the natural world, Carson might have chosen to adopt the strategy of arguing that insects and humans were *not* enemies and that war was the wrong metaphor to describe their relationship. To deconstruct the war metaphor as it was commonly applied to insects would have been a profoundly revolutionary move. Today's effort to reintroduce wolves on public lands, for example, has taken such an approach, reeducating the public to understand that wolves are not our enemies but are noble creatures whose presence enriches our lives. Carson, however, made only limited attempts to undermine the war metaphor by pointing out that there are good insects as well as bad insects and by questioning terms such as *weed* and *pest*. Her more dominant strategy is to agree with public sentiment that certain insects are indeed our enemies. Perhaps she sensed that it would have been impossible to persuade the public that gypsy moths, fire ants, and body lice are noble beings. She may have recognized that no amount of reeducation would convince a cotton grower that the boll weevil was not his enemy and that an attempt to do so would discredit her authority and alienate her audience.

## Carson as a Smart General

Leaving the war metaphor intact, Carson's strategy is to speak as a smart general, insisting that we are making some critical errors in the way that we are fighting this war, errors that may prove to be suicidal or that could cause the insects to win. One such error occurs, she says, when we turn powerful weapons against ourselves. The midwestern states, for example,

> have launched an attack [on the Japanese beetle] worthy of the most deadly enemy instead of only a moderately destructive insect, employing the most dangerous chemicals distributed in a manner that exposes large numbers of people, their domestic animals, and all wildlife to the poison intended for the beetle.

Another critical mistake is made repeatedly when our effort to eradicate a species backfires and actually strengthens that species, which rapidly evolves to become resistant to the chemical. While we are thus encouraging the evolution of superpests against which further chemical attacks are futile, our indiscriminate chemical barrage is simultaneously killing the natural predators of the pest species. As Carson writes, "[W]e have turned our artillery against our friends. The terrible danger is that we have grossly underestimated their value in keeping at bay a dark tide of enemies that, without their help, can overrun us." Carson thus concurs with an expert in soil science that "'a few false moves on the part of man . . . and the arthropods may well take over.'" As these dire warnings imply, Carson does not idealize insects but depicts them as a force to be reckoned with; consequently, we had better learn to fight more intelligently and forge some alliances.

Carson not only exposes the folly of prevailing insect-control strategies, she offers numerous smarter battle plans, including the importation of a given pest's natural predators, introduction of insect-specific diseases, release of sterilized males, various kinds of lures and traps, improved sanitation, new strains of pest-resistant crops, and greater diversity in plantings. She concludes, "There is, then, a whole battery of armaments available to the forester who is willing to look for permanent solutions that preserve and strengthen the natural relations in the forest." Carson promises no single solution, no atom bomb for insects, but rather recommends a variety of approaches, each depending on detailed, scientific knowledge of natural systems and each tailored to a specific situation. Just as America could not wipe out communism from the face of the earth but instead pursued a policy of containment and learned to establish diplomatic relations with a variety of Communist governments in many countries, so, too, Carson proposes that we seek not total extermination but rather "contain[ment] within reasonable bounds" and "a reasonable accommodation between the insect hordes and ourselves."

The foregoing discussion shows how Carson retains war-inflected language to propose a wiser defense plan against problem insects. War provides a readily comprehensible lens through which to view the relationship between humans and insects. The key is not to deny the war but to fight it more sensibly, with less risk to ourselves and our allies. While Carson thus agrees that certain insects are destructive, she argues that those very pests are less destructive to us than has been our chemical assault on them. Blanket spraying of potent synthetic chemicals poisons both humans and the natural systems upon which human life depends. Whoever is behind this rain of poisons is endangering our lives to a much greater degree than did the pest insects. By this clever move, Carson implies that the most deadly enemies are not the foreign insects but the insect controllers in our very midst. Such an accusation is tantamount to declaring a new war, a war between the pesticide industry and the people.

## A Bipolar World

There are many striking parallels between the rhetorics of the Cold War, *Silent Spring*, and modern environmentalism. Cold War rhetoric constructed a bipolar world, one in which two superpowers dominated the globe, with smaller countries falling under one or the other sphere of influence. Differences within each camp were minimized, while differences between the two camps were exaggerated. The possibility of a third, alternative position was denied. With only two choices, the question becomes simply, Which side are you on? As is typical of wartime rhetoric, the "other" side is portrayed as malevolent and aggressive, while "our" side is innocent and defensive. Scholars of Cold War rhetoric Lynn Boyd Hinds and Theodore Otto Windt, Jr., have documented how "the Soviets [were] transformed in this rhetoric of nihilation [negating] into subhuman monsters devoid of human feelings." Hinds and Windt explain that melodrama is a staple of wartime rhetoric, as a sinister villain menaces a helpless maiden who is in desperate need of a stalwart hero.

*Silent Spring* likewise creates a bipolar, melodramatic picture, with the pesticide industry and its henchmen in the Department of Agriculture on one side; Carson and a few heroic biologists and concerned citizens on the other; and with fainting nature and the unsuspecting American public costarring as damsels in distress. As Killingsworth and Palmer note,

> The agonistic [combative] exposé, of which *Silent Spring* is a fine example, . . . fosters controversy and divides perspectives, often attempting to arrange disparate interests into a clearly demarcated pair of opposed parties—environmentalist and developmentalist, for example—thus mobilizing citizens for a quick decision one way or the other.

Carson depicts "the control men" of the pesticide industry as inhuman, uncaring, and greedy. It is, in her words, "the authoritarian temporarily entrusted with power" who orders the spraying and thereby "disregard[s] supposedly inviolate property rights of private citizens" and "contaminate[s] the entire environment." "On every hand there is evidence that those engaged in spraying operations exercise a ruthless power," writes Carson. She observes that hers is "an era dominated by industry, in which the right to make a dollar at whatever cost is seldom challenged" and in which "nothing must get in the way of the man with the spray gun."

While the pesticide industry is clearly the villain, the public has been both a hapless victim of the "chemical death rain" and an unwitting accomplice by passively allowing such abuse to happen. Carson wrote *Silent Spring* in order to goad the passive to take action and to give the "many, many people who are eager to do something . . . the facts to *fight* with." (emphasis added). The rhetoric of bad guys (commonly portrayed as a powerful corporate minority) versus good guys (portrayed as the increasingly vocal majority) is a familiar feature of modern environmentalism.

During the Cold War, Winston Churchill's image of an Iron Curtain dividing Europe reinforced the sense of a bipolar world and, in addition, connoted that there were secret machinations taking place behind that Iron Curtain. As rhetoricians Hinds and Windt point out, this conception of mysterious dealings behind the curtain "pervaded interpretations of Soviet actions. Specific actions were never what they seemed, and one had to lift the masks from actors to interpret those actions for what they were." In other words, Soviet statements might be lies, and Soviet actions concealed ulterior motives.

Carson adopts this Iron Curtain approach by questioning what deals are struck behind the closed doors of the Department of Agriculture, of university research labs funded by the chemical industry, and in the board rooms of pesticide manufacturers. She warns that "the control men in state and federal governments—and of course the chemical manufacturers— . . . steadfastly deny the facts reported by the biologists and declare they see little evidence of harm to wildlife." Elsewhere, she refers to publications of the Department of Agriculture as "propaganda." Sen. Joseph McCarthy's announcement in 1950 that he had a list of 205 Communists working in the State Department probably had nothing to do with Carson's insinuation that there are environmental traitors within government; nonetheless, both accusations kindled public mistrust of government, and similar indictments of government officials are by now a commonplace of environmental rhetoric.

## An Unbridgeable Ideological Chasm

During the Cold War, statements from Washington rarely described tensions with the Soviet Union in the context of historical development or national interests; instead, the conflict was cast in ideological terms as a war between communism and capitalism, between totalitarianism and freedom. The ideological chasm separating the two great powers was assumed to be unbridgeable. Ultimately, the Cold War became a moral struggle between good and evil, lightness and darkness. The mutual mistrust and persistent focus on incompatible ideologies all but precluded compromise, dooming negotiations about important, pragmatic issues like arms reduction.

Carson, too, cast what could have been a pragmatic discussion of appropriate pesticide use into the more philosophical and ideological context of the proper relationship between humanity and nature. Paul Brooks notes that Rachel Carson knew that she would be attacked: "It was not simply that she was opposing indiscriminate use of poisons but—more fundamentally—that she had made clear the basic irresponsibility of an industrialized, technological society toward the natural world." Carson insists that the pesticide issue has a moral dimension: "Incidents like the eastern Illinois spraying raise a question that is not only scientific but moral. The question is whether any civilization can wage relentless war on life without . . . losing the right to be called civilized." As Carson represents this conflict, the unbridgeable ideological chasm is between domination and accommodation, arrogance and humility, stupidity and intelligence, greed and grace, right and wrong. Finding themselves publicly vilified, it is no wonder that chemical manufacturers attempted to block publication of the book and spent a quarter of a million dollars on a public-relations campaign. The ideological warfare of environmentalism continues today in much the same terms that Carson used, with a few new unbridgeable chasms appearing on the horizon, such as the ones separating patriarchy and ecofeminism, and anthropocentrism and biocentrism.

## A Climate of Crisis

Finally, and perhaps most important, both the Cold War and *Silent Spring* create a climate of crisis in order to justify their demand for drastic action. How was Truman to persuade Congress to spend millions of dollars to prop up corrupt governments like the one in Greece in 1947? He drew upon the public's memory of World War II to warn that, if Greece were to fall into the hands of the Communist revolutionaries, the rest of Europe could topple like dominoes. According to the rhetoric of the Cold War, as expressed by historian Louis Halle, the world stood at a crossroads in history: "'If the United States did not intervene now, all would be lost.'" Later, images of Armageddon were conjured up to pave the way for the quadrupling of the defense budget in 1950. In the blockade of Cuba in 1962, nothing less than national survival was said to be at stake. Hinds and Windt write, "In the medical world a crisis is a turning point for a sick patient, a crucial moment when a life or death decision must be made." They observe that Cold War rhetoric created a series of crises until an atmosphere of crisis became the consensus reality.

Just as Truman drew analogies between the Soviet Union and the Nazis, Carson exploited the leading fear of her time—the threat of nuclear war—to draw parallels between pesticides and radioactive fallout. The opening chapter of *Silent Spring* paints an imaginary picture of a pastoral American village suddenly afflicted with "a strange blight" that kills chickens, cattle, sheep, and even children at play. Carson then warns that a "grim specter has crept upon us almost unnoticed, and this imagined tragedy may easily become a stark reality we all shall know." Elsewhere she observes that "anything . . . within range of the chemical fallout may know the sinister touch of the poison." And because pesticides cause "a general and permanent lowering of environmental resistance," Carson predicts that "we may expect progressively more serious outbreaks of insects, both disease-carrying and crop-destroying species, in excess of anything we have ever known." In fact, she says, "[I]t is happening, here and now." She quotes a scientist, who confesses, "'We all live under the haunting fear that something may corrupt the environment to the point where man joins the dinosaurs as an obsolete form of life.'"

When, Carson asks, will the public demand action? Thanks to the wave of anxiety caused by *Silent Spring*, an answer would become: In the summer of '62. While initially doubtful that she would be able to penetrate the barrier of public indifference to so uncharismatic an issue as pesticides, Carson succeeded in finding just the right rhetorical formula to galvanize American citizens. By working within the Cold War paradigm of her day, substituting the pesticide industry for the Communist bloc as the purveyor of impending doom, Carson was able to tap into a powerful source of public energy and emotion.

## Questioning the Use of the War Metaphor

In part due to the precedent set by *Silent Spring*, the rhetoric of war, creating a climate of crisis, has been deployed by the environmental movement for more than three decades. One recent example from Dave Foreman's *Confessions of an Eco-Warrior* typifies the genre:

> We are living now in the most critical moment in the three-and-a-half-billion-year history of life on Earth. . . . Never before . . . has there been such a high rate of extinction as we are now witnessing. . . . Clearly, in such a time of *crisis*, the conservation *battle* is not one of merely *protecting* outdoor recreation opportunities, or a matter of aesthetics, or 'wise management and use' of natural resources. It is a *battle* for life itself.

The Cold War lasted for forty years. It will be interesting to see how long the consensus of environmental crisis can be maintained.

One goal of this essay has been to show how, having been catalyzed and colored by Rachel Carson's *Silent Spring*, the modern environmental movement has some of its roots in and continues to derive much of its rhetoric from war. In some cases, the clash between environmentalists and anti-environmentalists has escalated beyond mere rhetoric, as author David Helvarg documents in *The War Against the Greens*:

> [I]t is hard for me to imagine that environmental conflict in the United States might ever begin to resemble some of the haunting scenes of violence and hatred I had come to know as a war correspondent in Northern Ireland and Central America. But today, ... having seen the bomb and arson damage firsthand, and having met and talked to people who have been beaten, shot at and terrified, had their dogs mutilated, their cars run off the road, and their homes burned to the ground, I'm not so certain.

In the heat of the environmental backlash, perhaps it is time to question whether the trope of war—with its battles, its victories and defeats, its ecowarriors and enemies, its moral crusades and mortal fear—is an appropriate tool for solving environmental problems and making intelligent decisions. Perhaps in Carson's day, war was a necessary and appropriate context in which to conceptualize environmental issues. But, thankfully, the Cold War is over. Should people who are committed to enlightened stewardship of the earth continue to invoke it?

# Attacks on *Silent Spring* Were Gender Based

**Michael B. Smith**

*Michael B. Smith is assistant professor of history at Ithaca College. He has authored a number of articles on history and the environment.*

*In the following viewpoint, Smith posits that many of the attacks on Rachel Carson's book were based in emotion, rather than reason, and amounted to gender discrimination. In their vilification of Carson, Smith argues that the chemical industry and the patriarchal elite focused on attacking her as an uneducated and emotional woman because it was easier to do so, and better for public relations, than assailing the scientific basis of her work. Many critics attacked Carson's notion that nature and humanity must be balanced, arguing that humans would fall victim to the ravages of nature unless they mastered the environment. Smith relates that contemporary articles about Carson rarely showed her as a white-jacketed scientist: instead, they usually surrounded her with children or animals and characterized her as something of a schoolmarm. Carson's critics, Smith writes, accused her of attacking the very scientific breakthroughs that had made the good life in America safe and affordable.*

In their profoundly disturbing study of the public relations industry [*Trust Us, We're Experts*], John Stauber and Sheldon Rampton relate the story of how the public relations men for the chemical industry and the Department of Agriculture got wind of Carson's work even before its appearance in the *New Yorker*. By the end of the summer of 1962, when the book version of Carson's study was being prepared for press,

Michael B. Smith, "'Silence, Miss Carson!' Science, Gender, and the Reception of *Silent Spring*," *Feminist Studies*, vol. 27, no. 3, Fall 2001, pp. 736–744. Reproduced by permission of the author.

the anti-Carson machinery was already moving in high gear. [DDT manufacturer] Monsanto published a parody of *Silent Spring* in its in-house magazine that was entitled "The Desolate Year" and described a world overrun by insects. The Velsicol Chemical Corporation attempted to convince [book publisher] Houghton Mifflin not to publish the book at all, linking Carson to "food faddists" and other "fringe" groups. They also invoked the imperatives of the Cold War, contending that an overly credulous and uninformed public might call for the elimination of pesticides and that "our supply of food will be reduced to East-curtain parity." Finally, they threatened a libel suit against Carson's "innuendoes." None of these attempts to forestall the publication of *Silent Spring* was successful. So the chemical companies and other entities whose profit margins were threatened by Carson's findings resorted to counterattack through negative book reviews and opinion pieces in major periodicals. These attacks appeared in all forms of periodicals, from trade journals such as *Chemical and Engineering News* to popular news magazines such as *Time* and *U.S. News and World Report* to peer-reviewed science journals such as *Science*. The popularity and appeal of *Silent Spring* developed in spite of this barrage of discrediting assessments. But the rapid disappearance of the issue of pesticides from the national radar screen of public opinion by 1965; the assault on Rachel Carson herself, even in obituaries following her death from breast cancer in 1964; and the cheery "See, there were plenty of birds this spring" rejoinders that appeared in 1963 and 1964 all serve as suggestive, if not conclusive, evidence that the anti-Carson rhetoric did have a chilling effect on the discourse.

## Two Types of Critics

For the remainder of this . . . article I will examine the dissenting voices that sought to silence *Silent Spring*. These critics fell roughly into two categories. In the first were those who were members of the scientific community. The writers were almost all men. Almost all of them found the research undertaken by Carson for the book to be suspect; many of them questioned Carson's credentials, calling her an "amateur" or a mere "scientific journalist." Many also dismissed her writing as "emotional" and lacking the kind of cold, rational risk assessment required of modern applied science. Reading the reviews today one even senses some reviewers implicitly drawing a line between the "hard" science of chemistry and the "soft" science of biology. The second category of critics were from the popular press, the defenders of cold war-inflected notions of progress and justified means to ends. These writers also engaged in gendered critiques [based on Carson's being a woman] of what they called Carson's emotionalism and her vision of progress rooted in "sentimentalism" rather than reality. These critiques of *Silent Spring* appeared in magazines whose readership ranged across the spectrum, from *Good Housekeeping* to *Sports Illustrated* to *Life*. To be sure *Silent Spring* received numerous favorable reviews in the popular press. But even some of these reflected the gender biases noted above.

It is not surprising that some of the most vicious attacks on Rachel Carson and *Silent Spring* came from those with the greatest economic stake in the widespread use of chemical pesticides. As noted above, many chemical companies launched anti-Carson campaigns. But the reviews of *Silent Spring* that appeared in some of the trade journals reflected a hysteria that transcended even that which they accused Carson of. The most sexist, most unbalanced review of *Silent Spring* appeared in *Chemical and Engineering News* in October of 1962, shortly after the publication of the book. William Darby of the Vanderbilt University School of Medicine attacked Carson from the first paragraph of his review, entitled "Silence, Miss Carson!" The title itself (which the journal later admitted was its own creation, not Darby's) expresses the prevailing attitude among many of Carson's critics that she was an uninformed woman who was speaking of that which she knew not. Worse, she was speaking in a man's world, the inner sanctum of masculine science in which, like the sanctuary of a strict Calvinist sect, female silence was expected. Darby began his review by lumping Carson with groups he considered to be antimodern "freaks." *Silent Spring* would appeal to readers such as "the organic gardeners, the anti-fluoride leaguers, the worshippers of 'natural foods,' and those who cling to the philosophy of a vital principle, and pseudo-scientists and faddists," wrote Darby. He then invoked a series of father-figure scientists who supported the use of pesticides and whom Carson supposedly ignored. "It is doubtful that many readers can bear to wade through its high-pitched sequences of anxieties," Darby continued, impugning Carson's critical tone in terms all too reminiscent of sexist critiques of so-called feminine styles of discourse. But, Darby went on, if readers were moved by Carson's pleas and her invocation of [Franco-German physician Albert] Schweitzer and other critics of uncontrolled modernization, their view augured

> the end of all human progress, reversion to a passive social state devoid of technology, scientific medicine, agriculture, sanitation, or education. It means disease, epidemics, starvation, misery, and suffering incomparable and intolerable to modern man. Indeed, social, educational, and scientific development is prefaced on the conviction that man's lot will be and is being improved by greater understanding of and thereby increased ability to control or mold those forces responsible for man's suffering, misery, and deprivation. [English philosopher] Francis Bacon would have been proud of such a manifesto advocating *man's* role as conqueror, master, and controller of nature. Here we see not a judicious review of a controversial book but a defense of the ideology of modern science and progress against feminine sentimentality, the frightened growl of cornered dogma. Significantly, many readers of *Chemical and Engineering News* objected

passionately to Darby's characterization of Carson and *Silent Spring* in his review. But Darby was speaking as someone whose power was being undermined.

Another prominent male physician wrote an only slightly less corrosive review for a trade journal with a slightly different orientation, *Nutrition Reviews*. For Frederick J. Stare, Carson's "emotional picture" of a possible disaster disqualified her as a scientist and raised questions about her real commitment to humanity, for "the broad application of a brilliant technology" has allowed humanity to "stave off starvation, disease, and social and political unrest." Carson's interrogation of the application of science was, in Stare's mind, naive at best and unpatriotic at worst. Miss Carson, Stare concluded, was no scientist. Her use of phrases such as "never ending stream of chemicals . . . now pervading the world" and verbs such as "lurks" and "engulf" in reference to chemical residue consigned her to the role of sentimental essayist. Ignoring Carson's distinguished career as a marine biologist, Stare concluded: "In Miss Carson's case, research limited to selective reading, plus the urging of 'friends' with special interests, is certainly no diploma of equivalency for the academic training and experience required for authority."

Reviews and essays about *Silent Spring* that appeared in scientific journals did not contain such blatant attacks on Carson's character, although most were no less critical of her conclusions. Reviewer after reviewer—in all genre of periodicals—damned Carson's meddling in "progress," condemned her for proposing "unrealistic" alternatives. . . . [C]riticisms of Carson's science often alluded to her "soft" approach to a natural world that was humanity's adversary. There can be little doubt her belief that the "battle" with nature was not a zero-sum game, that our relationship with the nonhuman part of nature should not be characterized as a battle at all, threatened an entire sector of the economy whose profits were predicated on an adversarial formulation.

## Attacking the Balance of Nature

One conceit that Carson employed again and again in *Silent Spring* is "the balance of nature." Such a view of the natural world and the place of humanity in it raised the ire of [professor of agriculture] I.L. Baldwin, among others. In his 1962 review for *Science* Baldwin wrote: "It is certain that modern agriculture and modern public health, indeed, modern civilization, could not exist without an unrelenting war against the return of a true balance of nature." Like Darby, Baldwin deployed the assertion that from science had sprung modernity, that alternatives to the existing practice of science were antimodern and would inevitably result in casting humanity back in the cauldron of competition with the rest of the natural world, a nature red in tooth and claw. Besides, Baldwin wrote, "The problem Rachel Carson dramatizes is not a new one"; competent men were working within the dominant scientific paradigm to make necessary corrections. "[Their] reports are not dramatically written, and they were not intended to be best sellers. They are, however, the result of careful study by a wide group of scientists, and they represent balanced judgements in areas in which emotional appeals tend to overbalance sound judgement based on facts." Rachel Carson's science, then, was "unbalanced" and "emotional." Restraint—that is, protecting the status quo—was the most "rational" course. Others criticized Carson in a similar vein. Her use of the image of a "fragile and exquisite songbird dying in paralytic convulsions" was, according to Thomas H. Jukes in *American Scientist*, an unforgivably sentimental tactic for raising awareness about the issue of "possible" pesticide misuse. Jukes condemned those followers of [nineteenth-century environmentalist] John Muir who want to see his vision of pure nature preserved but would not "adopt his diet of tea and bread crusts," those hypocritical idealists who want to have both modernity and a balance of nature: not possible, he flatly asserted. (I.L Baldwin had made a similar claim, stating that the elimination or even significant reduction of pesticides would mean a "back-to-the-farm migration for millions.")

These writers and others were trying to preserve the public's credulity in the ability of science and technology to solve problems both presented by nature and those that developed as unforeseen consequences of applied science. Even one of the more balanced reviews of *Silent Spring* in a scientific magazine had this agenda at its core. "I suspect that the inevitable way to progress for man, as for nature," wrote [Cornell University professor] LaMont C. Cole in *Scientific American*, "is to try new things in an almost haphazard manner, discarding the failures and building upon the successes." It was just this blind faith Carson was trying to shake. The *New York Times* opined even before her book appeared that "she warns of the dangers of misuse and overuse by a public that has become mesmerized by the notion that chemists are the possessors of divine wisdom and that nothing but benefit can emerge from their test tubes."

## Attacking an Emotional Woman

That a woman should challenge the mesmerists, that she should try to shake Americans from their complacent trust in their own government and most powerful corporations, dismayed not just the chemical companies and their colleagues in research universities. Her *New Yorker* pieces drew overwhelming praise from readers, but a vocal minority objected to her and her findings strenuously. One writer wrote: "Miss Rachel Carson's reference to the selfishness of insecticide manufacturers probably reflects her Communist sympathies, like a lot of our writers these days. We can live without birds and animals, but, as the current market slump shows, we cannot live without business. As for insects, isn't it just like a woman to be scared to death of a few little bugs! As long as we have the H-bomb everything will be O.K."

*A World War II-era poster encouraging the use of chemical pesticides on home gardens. Critics of* Silent Spring *argued that the work attacked the scientific advancements that had made produce in America safe and affordable since the Industrial Revolution.* © Swim Ink 2, LLC/Corbis.

If letters from cranks had been the extent of the public complaints against Carson in the popular press, one could less confidently assert that gender biases from the culture at large deeply inflected the reception of her work. But when a magazine with the wide readership of *Time* called her findings and writing "patently unsound," "hysterically emphatic," and an "emotional outburst," then the roots of the criticism, the reasons Carson was so threatening, become clear: she was a woman and she was challenging a cornerstone of industrial capitalism with a passion considered unbecoming to a scientist. The *Time* piece also trotted out the familiar criticism about the "balance of nature": "Lovers of wildlife often rhapsodize about the 'balance of nature' that keeps all living creatures in harmony, but scientists realistically point out that the balance of nature was upset thousands of years ago when man's invention of weapons made him the king of the beasts. The balance has never recovered its equilibrium; man is the dominant species on his planet, and as his fields, pastures and cities spread across the land, lesser species are extirpated, pushed into refuge areas, or domesticated."

The Catholic periodical of record, *America*, also savaged *Silent Spring*, again noting Carson's "emotionalism" and lack of balance. *The National Review* called the book "simply a long emotional attack," Carson's approach "emotional and one-sided," an "obscurantist appeal to the emotions." Again invoking the need for "rational" and "scientific" (as opposed to emotional or irrational and sentimental) approach, the review concluded by saying that "[the problem of pesticides] is Burkean, and involves a careful weighing of advantages and disadvantages with due regard to our lack of perfect knowledge." *Newsweek* wondered about the critics' view of *Silent Spring* as "innuendo" and having "the quality of gossip." "Her extravagant language . . . , her unscientific use of innuendo . . . , her pantheism [belief that nature and the Deity are identical] . . . , and her disregard for the studies of the problem by her fellow scientists in industry, the university, and government service" (mostly men of course) rendered her study completely unreliable, commented another reviewer. Even a profile of Carson in *Life* purporting to be a balanced assessment of the woman and her work could not overlook the implications of Carson's sex noting that "for all her gentle mien [manner], Rachel Carson, 55, who is unmarried but not a feminist . . . is a formidable adversary." This phrase suggests that were Carson a feminist she would indeed be a subversive force, for (with a wink to the reader) *Life* subscribers all know what *those* women are like. And yet there is also in these words the implication that Carson's unmarried status is itself an expression of some deficiency, that were she married, none of this controversy would have developed. Presumably she would have instead been practicing home economics and recognizing the overwhelming benefits of pesticide-enhanced agricultural bounty for the kitchen. There is, in fact, no evidence to suggest Carson openly advocated for women's rights, although her own struggle with the scientific establishment served as a feminist statement. By the second page of the profile Carson had morphed into a pesky gadfly, a "good indignant crusader." Finally, the article concluded, like troublesome Mother Nature herself, "Hurricane Rachel" must be endured, becalmed, and then "the real dangers to public health [could] be evaluated, and then controlled by skilled medical men."

Like many of the articles about Carson and *Silent Spring* the *Life* profile featured photographs of Carson, few of which depicted her in the guise of a professional scientist. There were none of the usual press release photographs of a white-coated notable scientist in the lab looking authoritative or the dauntless field researcher above the volcano's mouth. Instead, Carson was almost always photographed with her cat or sitting in the woods surrounded by children gesturing at the natural wonders of the world. Only occasionally did a photo of her at a microscope appear. By implication, these photos located Carson in the world of the school marm, not the world of science. She was a teacher—to some a subversive, dangerous one—but not someone who was engaged in meaningful scientific research.

Even one year after the publication of the book, even after a commission appointed by President [John F.] Kennedy had sustained many of Carson's conclusions about pesticides, the assault on Carson in print continued. An early collaborator on *Silent Spring*, Edwin Diamond, described how he simply could not work with a woman who let emotion interfere with accuracy and whose final product relied on the same shock techniques and distortions employed by Joseph McCarthy. The story, "Life-Giving Spray" (featuring the obligatory photograph of Carson as sentimental bird watcher), appeared in the quintessential male magazine, *Sports Illustrated*, and concluded that one year after Carson's frightening indictment wildlife seemed more abundant than ever, and was, in fact, aided by pesticide use.

## Preserving Scientific Dominance

Even the airwaves were filled with vilification of Carson, critiques once again suffused with gendered notions of science and who does "good" science. In a widely distributed speech of January 1963, the president of the Nutrition Foundation, C.G. King, like Frederick Stare and others cited above, condemned Carson as a fellow traveler with all of the fringe elements of society: "Food faddists, health quacks, and special interest groups are promoting her book as if it were scientifically irreproachable and written by a scientist. Neither is true . . . and [Carson] misses the very essence of science in not being objective either in citing the evidence or in its interpretation." The frequently interviewed Robert H. White-Stevens, whose British accent and grandfatherly appearance evidently conferred upon him a trustworthiness unmerited by his intemperate remarks, proved to be the king of anti-Carson sound bites with variations on the following characterization of *Silent Spring*: "Her book is littered with crass assumptions and gross misinterpretations, misquotations, and misunderstandings, clearly calculated to mislead the uninformed. . . . Her book will come to be regarded in time as a gross distortion of the actual facts, essentially unsupported by either scientific experimental evidence or practical experience in the field." For these men, whose power in shaping society through expert scientific advice hung on their credibility as both protectors of the public interest and exemplars of "true" science, Rachel Carson's conclusions and analysis were terrifying. Carson's critics—mostly men, mostly white, mostly affiliated with some bureaucratic institution—recognized the general public's willingness to accept science as it was being practiced as the ultimate authority. They therefore took two approaches to discrediting her, both of which often led the reader to make inferences about how gender inflected her science and both of which sought to shore up the foundations of science that Carson's critique of modernity had shaken. Carson's critics tried to reassure the world that even if some of what Carson alleged was true, the mistakes resulted from misapplication, not misguided science. Science, they argued, was almost solely responsible for the extraordinary standard of living Americans were experiencing by the early 1960s. To heed Carson's warnings would be tantamount to killing the goose that was laying the golden egg. Since the Progressive Era [1890s to 1920s] when the federal government had begun regulating society in earnest for the first time, the burgeoning American middle class had been willing to accept safety regulations only to the extent that such regulations did not incur large increases in the price of consumer goods. As was the case with the meat-packing industry in the first decade of the twentieth century following the publication of [US author] Upton Sinclair's *The Jungle*, those who stood to profit directly from the heavy use of pesticides responded to *Silent Spring* with the consumer's wallet in mind, thereby striking a putative balance—if it can be called such a thing—between public health safety and affordability. "[Because of pesticides] today's American housewives have the widest choice of fruits and vegetables, and meats and dairy—at prices to fit their budgets," characterizes this rhetoric.

# Silent Spring Does Not Begin or End the Battle over Pesticide Policy

*Rachel Carson*

*Rachel Carson, the author of* Silent Spring, *is generally regarded as one of the founders of the environmental movement.*

*In the following viewpoint, a speech given to a garden society in 1963, Rachel Carson defends* Silent Spring *against its critics and argues that her book is only a part of the ongoing struggle against the indiscriminant spraying of what she argues should be termed "biocides" and not "pesticides." She also reiterates the problems with chemical pest controls that she outlined in* Silent Spring, *observes that the public concern her book has awakened is a hopeful sign, and urges her listeners to continue to be vigilant in their opposition to the spraying of chemicals. Citing global examples of where chemical agriculture has caused widespread disease, Carson implores her audience to understand that such outbreaks could happen in the United States. She concludes by stating that when her audience considers the controversy surrounding her book, they should always take into account who is speaking and the nature of that speaker's agenda.*

I am particularly glad to have this opportunity to speak to you. Ever since, ten years ago, you honored me with your Frances Hutchinson medal, I have felt very close to the Garden Club of America. And I should like to pay tribute to you for the quality of your work and for the aims and aspirations of your organization. Through your interest in plant life, your

Rachel Carson, "The Publication of *Silent Spring* Was Neither the Beginning Nor the End of That Struggle: Speech to the Garden Club of America, New York, NY, January 8, 1963," *Speaking of Earth: Environmental Speeches That Moved the World*, edited by Alon Tal, New Brunswick, NJ, and London: Rutgers University Press, 2006, pp. 7–13. Copyright © 2006 by Alon Tal. Reprinted by permission of Rutgers University Press.

fostering of beauty, your alignment with constructive conservation causes, you promote that onward flow of life that is the essence of our world.

## Destructive Forces

This is a time when forces of a very different nature too often prevail—forces careless of life or deliberately destructive of it and of the essential web of living relationships. My particular concern, as you know, is with the reckless use of chemicals so unselective in their action that they should more appropriately be called biocides rather than pesticides. Not even their most partisan defenders can claim that their toxic effect is limited to insects or rodents or weeds or whatever the target may be.

The battle for a sane policy for controlling unwanted species will be a long and difficult one. The publication of *Silent Spring* was neither the beginning nor the end of that struggle. I think, however, that it is moving into a new phase, and I would like to assess with you some of the progress that has been made and take a look at the nature of the struggle that lies before us.

We should be very clear about what our cause is. What do we oppose? What do we stand for? If you read some of my industry-oriented reviewers, you will think that I am opposed to efforts to control insects or other organisms. This, of course, is *not* my position and I am sure it is not that of the Garden Club of America. We differ from the promoters of biocides chiefly in the means we advocate, rather than the end to be attained.

It is my conviction that if we automatically call in the spray planes or reach for the aerosol bomb when we have an insect problem we are resorting to crude methods of a rather low scientific order. We are being particularly unscientific when we fail to press forward with research that will give us the new kind of weapons we need. Some such weapons now exist—brilliant and imaginative prototypes of what I trust will be the insect control methods of the future. But we need many more, and we need to make better use of those we have. Research men of the Department of Agriculture have told me privately that some of the measures they have developed and tested and turned over to the insect control branch have been quietly put on the shelf.

## Problems with Chemical Controls

I criticize the present heavy reliance upon biocides on several grounds—first, on the grounds of their inefficiency. I have here some comparative figures on the toll taken of our crops by insects before and after the DDT era. During the first half of this century, crop loss due to insect attack has been estimated by a leading entomologist [scientist who studies insects] at 10 percent a year. It is startling to find then, that the National Academy of Science last year placed the present crop loss at 25 percent a year. If the percentage of crop loss is increasing at this rate, even as the use of modern insecticides increases, surely something is wrong with the methods used! I would remind you that a nonchemical method gave 100 percent control of the screwworm fly—a degree of success no chemical has ever achieved.

Chemical controls are inefficient also because as now used they promote resistance among insects. The number of insect species resistant to one or more group of insecticides has risen from about a dozen in pre-DDT days to nearly 150 today. This is a very serious problem, threatening, as it does, greatly impaired control.

Another measure of inefficiency is the fact that chemicals often provoke resurgence of the very insect they seek to control, because they have killed off its natural controls. Or they cause some other organism suddenly to rise to nuisance status: spider mites, once relatively innocuous, have become a worldwide pest since the advent of DDT.

Obviously, it will take time to revolutionize our methods of insect and weed control to the point where dangerous chemicals are minimized. Meanwhile, there is much that can be done to bring about some immediate improvement in the situation through better procedures and controls.

## Greater Awareness Has Been a Positive Outcome

In looking at the pesticide situation today, the most hopeful sign is an awakening of strong public interest and concern. People are beginning to ask questions and to insist upon proper answers instead of meekly acquiescing in whatever spraying programs are proposed. This in itself is a wholesome thing.

There is increasing demand for better legislative control of pesticides. The state of Massachusetts has already set up a Pesticide Board with actual authority. This board has taken a very necessary step by requiring the licensing of anyone proposing to carry out aerial spraying. Incredible though it may seem, before this was done anyone who had money to hire an airplane could spray where and when he pleased. I am told that the state of Connecticut is now planning an official investigation of spraying practices. And of course, on a national scale, the president [John F. Kennedy] last summer directed his science advisor to set up a committee of scientists to review the whole matter of the government's activities in this field.

Citizen groups too, are becoming active. For example, the Pennsylvania Federation of Women's Clubs recently set up a program to protect the public from the menace of poisons in the environment—a program based on education and promotion of legislation. The National Audubon Society has advocated a five-point action program involving both state and federal agencies. The North American Wildlife Conference this year will devote an important part of its program to the problem of pesticides. All these developments will serve to keep public attention focused on the problem.

I was amused recently to read a bit of wishful thinking in one of the trade magazines. Industry "can take heart" it said, "from the fact that the main impact of the book (i.e., *Silent Spring*) will occur late in the fall and winter—seasons when consumers are not normally active buyers of insecticides. . . . It is fairly safe to hope that by March or April *Silent Spring* no longer will be an interesting conversational subject."

If the tone of my mail from readers is any guide, and if the movements that have already been launched gain the expected momentum, this is one prediction that will not come true.

## Avoiding Complacency Is the Key to Success

This is not to say that we can afford to be complacent. Although the attitude of the public is showing a refreshing change there is very little evidence of any reform in spraying practices. Very toxic materials are being applied with solemn official assurances that they will harm neither man nor beast. When wildlife losses are later reported, the same officials deny the evidence or declare the animals must have died from "something else."

Exactly this pattern of events is occurring in a number of areas now. For example, a newspaper in East St. Louis, Illinois, describes the death of several hundred rabbits, quail, and song-birds in areas treated with pellets of the insecticide dieldrin. One area involved was, ironically, a "game preserve." This was part of a program of Japanese beetle control.

The procedures seem to be the same as those I described in *Silent Spring*, referring to another Illinois community, Sheldon. At Sheldon, the destruction of many birds and small mammals amounted almost to annihilation. Yet an Illinois Agriculture official is now quoted as saying dieldrin has no serious effect on animal life.

A significant case history is shaping up now in Norfolk, Virginia. The chemical is the very toxic dieldrin, the target the white-fringed beetle, which attacks some farm crops. This situation has several especially interesting features. One is the evident desire of the state agriculture officials to carry out the program with as little advance discussion as possible. When the Outdoor Edition of the *Norfolk Virginian-Pilot* "broke" the story, it reported that officials refused comment on their plans. The Norfolk health officer offered reassuring statements to the public, on the grounds that the method of application guaranteed safety: The poison would be injected into the ground by a machine that drills holes in the soil. "A child would have to eat the roots of the grass to get the poison," he is quoted as saying.

However, alert reporters soon proved these assurances to be without foundation. The actual method of application was to be by seeders, blowers, and helicopters: the same type of procedure that in Illinois wiped out robins, brown thrashers, and meadowlarks, killed sheep in the pastures, and contaminated the forage so that cows gave milk containing poison.

Yet, at a hearing of sorts, concerned Norfolk citizens were told merely that the state's Department of Agriculture was committed to the program and that it would therefore be carried out. The fundamental wrong is that authoritarian control has been vested in the agricultural agencies. There are, after all, many different interests involved: there are problems of water pollution, of soil pollution, of wildlife protection, of public health. Yet the matter is approached as if the agricultural interests were the supreme, or indeed the only, one.

It seems to me clear that all such problems should be resolved by a conference of representatives of all the interests involved.

If we are ever to find our way out of the present deplorable situation, we must remain vigilant, we must continue to challenge and to question, we must insist that the burden of proof is on those who would use these chemicals to prove the procedures are safe.

Above all, we must not be deceived by the enormous stream of propaganda that is issuing from the pesticide manufacturers and from industry-related—although ostensibly independent—organizations. There is already a large volume of handouts openly sponsored by the manufacturers. There are other packets of materials being issued by some of the state agricultural colleges, as well as by certain organizations whose industry connections are concealed behind a scientific front. This material is going to writers, editors, professional people, and other leaders of opinion.

## Chemical Use Could Cause Tragedies in the United States

It is characteristic of this material that it deals in generalities, unsupported by documentation. In its claims for safety to human beings, it ignores the fact that we are engaged in a grim experiment never before attempted. We are subjecting whole populations to exposure to chemicals which animal experiments have proved to be extremely poisonous and in many cases cumulative in their effect. These exposures now begin at or before birth. No one knows what the result will be, because we have no previous experience to guide us.

Let us hope it will not take the equivalent of another thalidomide tragedy to shock us into full awareness of the hazard. Indeed, something almost as shocking has already occurred: a few months ago we were all shocked by newspaper accounts of the tragedy of the Turkish children who have developed a horrid disease through use of an agricultural chemical. To be sure, the use was unintended. The poisoning has been continuing over a period of some seven years, unknown to most of us. What made it newsworthy in 1962 was the fact that a scientist gave a public report on it.

A disease known as toxic porphyria has turned some five thousand Turkish children into hairy, monkey-faced beings. The skin becomes sensitive to light and is blotched and blistered. Thick hair covers much of the face and arms. The victims have also suffered severe liver damage. Several hundred such cases were noticed in 1955. Five years later, when a South African physician visited Turkey to study the disease, he found five thousand victims. The cause was traced to seed wheat, which had been treated with a chemical fungicide called hexachlorobenzene. The seed, intended for planting, had instead been ground into flour for bread by the hungry people. Recovery of the victims is slow, and indeed worse may be in store for them. Dr. W. C. Hueper, a specialist on environmental cancer, tells me there is a strong likelihood these unfortunate children may ultimately develop liver cancer.

"This could not happen here," you might easily think. It would surprise you, then, to know that the use of poisoned seed in our own country is a matter of present concern by the Food and Drug Administration. In recent years there has been a sharp increase in the treatment of seed with chemical fungicides and insecticides of a highly poisonous nature. Two years ago an official for the Food and Drug Administration told me of that agency's fear that treated grain left over at the end of a growing season was finding its way into food channels.

Now, on last October 27, the Food and Drug Administration proposed that all treated food grain seed be brightly colored so as to be easily distinguishable from untreated seeds or grain intended as food for human beings or livestock. . . .

## Commercial Entities Present Obstacles to Progress

I understood, however, that objection has been made by some segments of the industry and that this very desirable and necessary requirement may be delayed. This is a specific example of the kind of situation requiring public vigilance and public demand for correction of abuses.

The way is not made easy for those who would defend the public interest. In fact, a new obstacle has recently been created, and a new advantage has been given to those who seek to block remedial legislation. I refer to the income tax bill which becomes effective this year. The bill contains a little known provision which permits certain lobbying expenses to be considered a business expense deduction. It means, to cite a specific example, that the chemical industry may now work at bargain rates to thwart future attempts at regulation.

But what of the nonprofit organizations such as the garden clubs, the Audubon Societies, and all other such tax-exempt groups? Under existing laws they stand to lose their tax-exempt status if they devote any "substantial" part of their activities to attempts to influence legislation. The word "substantial" needs to be defined. In practice, even an effort involving less than 5 percent of an organization's activity has been ruled sufficient to cause loss of the tax-exempt status.

What happens then, when the public interest is pitted against large commercial interests? Those organizations wishing to plead for protection of the public interest do so under the peril of losing the tax-exempt status so necessary to their existence. The industry wishing to pursue its course without legal restraint is now actually subsidized in its efforts.

This is a situation which the Garden Club and similar organizations, within their legal limitations, might well attempt to remedy.

There are other disturbing factors, which I can only suggest. One is the growing interrelation between professional organizations and industry, and between science and industry. For example, the American Medical Association, through its newspaper, has referred physicians to a pesticide trade association for information to help them answer patients' questions about the effects of pesticides on man. I would like to see physicians referred to authoritative scientific or medical literature, not to a trade organization whose business is to promote the sale of pesticides.

We see scientific societies acknowledging as "sustaining associates" a dozen or more giants of a related industry. When the scientific organization speaks, whose voice do we hear, that of science or of the sustaining industry? The public assumes it is hearing the voice of science.

Another cause of concern is the increasing size and number of industry grants to the universities. On first thought, such support of education seems desirable, but on reflection we see that this does not make for unbiased research; it does not promote a truly scientific spirit. To an increasing extent, the man who brings the largest grants to his university becomes an untouchable, with whom even the university president and trustees do not argue.

These are large problems and there is no easy solution. But the problems must be faced.

As you listen to the present controversy about pesticides, I recommend that you ask yourself: Who speaks? And Why?

# Silent Spring Challenges Our Commitment to Environmental Safety

*Marla Cone*

*Marla Cone is an environmental reporter at the* Los Angeles Times *and the author of* Silent Snow: The Slow Poisoning of the Arctic.

*In the following viewpoint, Cone notes that when she began covering environmental issues as a writer in the 1980s, she thought* Silent Spring *was no longer relevant. Cone came to realize, she reports, that the buildup of chemicals in the environment that Carson wrote about continues unabated to this day. Though Carson's purposely exaggerated "Fable for Tomorrow" never came true, Cone asserts that the lingering effects of chemical buildup in the environment are still not known. Cone wonders what effects these chemicals have had on children. The argument for environmental vigilance, therefore, is not to prevent a doomsday scenario, Cone concludes. The real question is whether humans want to prevent the more subtle, insidious consequences of a lackadaisical environmental policy.*

As a crop-duster swooped down over a row of vegetables in [Southern] California's Imperial Valley, I sat in a pickup truck, the windows rolled up. It was the spring of 1997 and I was investigating a story about efforts by Native American tribes to outlaw aerial spraying of pesticides. I was also five months pregnant, and when I embarked on the trip I rationalized that if I happened to be exposed to a single, minuscule dose of a pesticide, it wasn't going to do any harm. But at that moment, alone in the darkness, parked on a dirt road next to the field, I was having second thoughts.

Marla Cone, "The Unbroken Chain," *Columbia Journalism Review*, vol. 44, no. 2, 2005, pp. 65–68. Reproduced by permission.

I knew that the fetus I was carrying was the most vulnerable life on Earth when it came to the dangers of pesticides and other toxic chemicals. Was this story worth the risk—any risk, no matter how small? As I watched the plane unleash a trail of diluted insecticide, I noticed a fly inside the cab buzzing against the windshield. I decided that if it suddenly fell silent, I would start the ignition and take off. As absurd as it seems now, watching that fly manage to survive calmed me. At the time I chalked it up to the irrational obsession of a pregnant woman, but I now realize that the fly was my totem, a symbol straight out of Rachel Carson's *Silent Spring*.

## The "Chain of Evil" Persists

Oddly enough, when I began covering environmental problems in the mid-1980s, I thought that *Silent Spring* was an anachronism, important only as a reminder of people's profound ignorance about the environment during the post-World War II industrial age. I was starting kindergarten in September of 1962 when Carson published her epic warning about how man-made pesticides were poisoning the world. Oblivious to what Carson called the "elixirs of death," I grew up on the shoreline of Lake Michigan, in one of the nation's toxic hotspots, Waukegan, Illinois, and during the time when the "Dirty Dozen"—the ubiquitous DDT and other toxic chlorinated chemicals—were reaching record levels in all our urban environments, particularly around the Great Lakes. Yet by the time I was a teenager in the 1970s, the world's worst environmental problems had supposedly been brought under control. We had seen the Evil Empire and it was that of our fathers and mothers. We were the offspring of the clueless World War II generation that sprayed DDT and poisoned the Great Lakes and fouled the air. We were finding the solution to pollution.

But I now realize that what Carson called the "chain of evil"—the buildup of chemicals in our environment—continues unbroken to this day. And even though the political firestorm Carson's book stirred up forty-three years ago burns with just as much intensity today, most of Carson's science remains sound and her warnings prescient. If we take a mental snapshot of what we know now about the dangers of chemical exposure, the questions still outnumber the answers. Yet one thing remains as certain as it was in 1962: we are leaving a toxic trail that will outlive us.

The first chapter of *Silent Spring*, "Fable for Tomorrow," is one of the grimmest scenes in American literature, fact or fiction. "There was once a town in the heart of America where all life seemed to live in harmony with its surrounding," Carson begins. It was a glorious place. Birds chirped, fish jumped, foxes barked, trees and flowers were ablaze with color. "Then a strange blight crept over the area and everything began to change," she continues. Robins, jays, and scores of other songbirds disappeared, livestock were sickened, trees and flowers withered, streams were lifeless, children dropped dead suddenly while playing. "No witchcraft, no enemy action had silenced the rebirth of new life in this stricken world," Carson explains. "The people had done it themselves."

No such town actually existed. "But it might easily have a thousand counterparts in America or elsewhere in the world," Carson writes.

A nature writer and aquatic biologist with the U.S. Fish and Wildlife Service, Carson had already written two best sellers before she spent four years researching *Silent Spring*. She described in great scientific detail the dangers of DDT and its sister chlorinated chemicals, and her writings transformed how people felt about pesticides. After World War II, synthetic compounds were being invented on a daily basis, especially after the wonders of combining carbon and chlorine molecules had been discovered. DDT was fast synthesized in the 1800s, and it was used in great volumes as an insecticide beginning in the 1940s. Its power was thought to be extraordinary because, although it killed bugs, it wasn't acutely poisonous and seemed relatively benign to everything but bugs. Soon, though, it became clear that DDT was dangerous in a slow, insidious sort of way. In the 1950s and 1960s, it began spreading world-wide, building up in oceans, waterways, and soil. It didn't easily break down in the environment, remaining in the food chain for decades. It collected in fat and tissues, passing from one animal to another—from plankton to worm to fish to bird, from hay to cow to milk to human child.

*Silent Spring* explained all that, and it became a phenomenal best seller. No other environmental book has had such a far-reaching impact. Carson was a scientist, a journalist, and a crusader, and her book scared the hell out of people. She portrayed the science of the day in such dense detail that much of the 368-page book is too unwieldy, even today, for most readers to comprehend. Yet her gift as a writer was her eloquent and shocking prose, in which she philosophized about the ramifications of the science. Her words hastened the dawn of the environmental movement in the late 1960s, and by the early 1970s, the United States and most of the developed world had banned DDT and many other chlorinated compounds.

Carson's fabled world of the future, of course, has not materialized. But what's remarkable now when I reread *Silent Spring* is that the reality Carson described remains our own. DDT, PCBs [toxic organic compounds], and related compounds remain in the tissues of virtually every living thing. They continue to spread globally, from pole to pole, via the air and ocean currents. Even eagles' eggs on Alaska's remote Aleutian Islands contain high levels of DDT despite the fact that the pesticide has never been sprayed there.

## Carson Demonized

When the manuscript of *Silent Spring* was serialized in *The New Yorker* in June 1962, Carson was demonized. Chemical companies, and even some of her fellow scientists, attacked her data and interpretations, lambasted her credentials', called her hysterical and one-sided, and pressured her publisher, Houghton Mifflin, to withdraw *Silent Spring*. [The chemical corporation] Monsanto went so far as to publish a parody of *Silent Spring*, called "The Desolate Year," in which famine, disease, and insects take over the world after pesticides have been banned.

Carson is still the target of countless critiques. "DDT killed bald eagles because of its persistence in the environment. *Silent Spring* is now killing African children because of its persistence in the public mind," [Pulitzer Prize–winning journalist] Tina Rosenberg wrote last year in a piece about malaria in *The New York Times Magazine* called "What the World Needs Now Is DDT." It's true that *Silent Spring* failed to describe the benefits of pesticides in fighting malaria, which is spread by mosquitoes, and in protecting food crops from destructive pests. Perhaps Carson believed that everyone acknowledged the benefits while ignoring the risks. Her goal, after all, was action, not contemplation.

Nevertheless, accusing *Silent Spring* of killing children in Africa is disingenuous. Most malaria experts including the Malaria Foundation international, aren't rallying behind DDT. They support its limited use only until cost-effective substitutes are in place, perhaps in a few years. DDT remains one of the few cheap, effective tools used in the war against malaria, which kills more than two million people a year, mostly children in Africa. But unlike the 1950s and 1960s, when up to 400,000 tons a year were sprayed from trucks and airplanes, the current practice is to spray only the interior walls of houses at risk.

## A Personal Heart of Darkness

When Carson was writing, it was considered cutting-edge science to determine whether a chemical mutated cells or triggered tumors, which explains why *Silent Spring* emphasizes the cancer risk of chemical compounds, a claim that looks a bit outdated today. Carson also had a personal reason for her warnings about carcinogens. She was diagnosed with breast cancer while writing *Silent Spring*, and it killed her at the age of fifty-six [Carson technically died of heart disease], less than two years after her book was published. Today there is little evidence of a link between DDT in women's bodies and the rate of breast cancer. Nevertheless, the cancer link has not been dismissed. Scientists wonder if brief exposure to DDT and other chemicals in the womb, rather than the amounts accumulated over a lifetime, can trigger cancer later in life.

Unbeknownst to Carson, chemicals at low doses have even more insidious dangers, beyond cancer. Scientists now believe that many industrial compounds and pesticides, including DDT, assault the innermost workings of living things— skewing brain development, sex hormones, and immune cells.

Carson accused those who extolled the virtues of pesticides of dispensing "little tranquilizing pills of half truth" and "sugar coating" unpalatable facts. "The public must decide whether it wishes to continue on the present road," she insisted, "and it can do so only when in full possession of the facts."

As a journalist, I know that is where I come in. For Carson, suffering from cancer, *Silent Spring* was her own personal heart of darkness, an excruciating journey into her own mind and the "sinister" world of chemicals. For me, writing about chemicals provokes its own inner turmoil as I seek certainty in an age of ambiguity. How do we square the risks of a chemical with its benefits? The precautionary principle, codified by the European Union, prescribes preventive measures when science is uncertain. The American philosophy prefers after-the-fact fixes rather than precautionary steps that may be excessive.

*Crews excavating soil contaminated with DDT and arsenic at the former site of Chemical Insecticide Corp. in Edison, New Jersey, 2005. The location became notorious in the 1990s when rabbits were discovered in the area with green-tinged fur, leading the federal government to declare it a Superfund site.* © AP Images/Mike Derer.

## Fear Versus Boredom

I was once accused of writing with "too much of the gravity of Rachel Carson." I wonder whether that's a weakness or a strength. After all, newspapers today tend to simplify issues related to environmental health and publish pieces that tell readers essentially nothing. We shouldn't unjustifiably scare readers, but we shouldn't bore them either. Most environmental journalists writing about toxic chemicals do one or the other. Those who bore readers haven't done the homework to understand the risks of certain chemicals and consequently are incapable of explaining those risks in terms people can understand. Those who scare readers don't put the risks in perspective or fail to reveal which chemicals and which exposures matter the most. We don't have to write with the grim foreboding of *Silent Spring* or the intentional exaggeration of its "Fable for Tomorrow," or ignore the benefits of the chemicals we rely upon today. But we do need to master Carson's skill for explaining what is at stake.

Carson's readers reacted with outrage, but many people today seem to prefer to remain ignorant of the risks of the chemicals they are routinely exposed to. "It is human nature to shrug off what may seem to us a vague threat of future disaster," Carson asserted, and that, in part, explains why the American mindset remains closer to "better living through chemistry" than "better safe than sorry." I behave like any American consumer. I have resorted to sprinkling diazinon on anthills and passing over organic foods because they cost too much. I'm aware that my new mattress contains flame retardants and my nail polish has phthalates, but I bought them anyway. I haven't tossed out my polycarbonate food containers, and recently when my dentist filled a cavity, I chose an amalgam that contains a trace of mercury because it is more durable than the mercury-free alternatives.

## New Challenges

Still, after nineteen years on the beat, I certainly know that the fly buzzing at the windshield was not a valid way to assess the dangers of pesticide exposure. When it comes to low doses we encounter in our daily lives, there are no dead bodies, no smoking guns. Many scientists now say the effects on children's brains and reproductive and immune systems are subtle, virtually impossible to pin down. Sometimes I think back to family dinners at a popular fish restaurant at Waukegan Harbor [Illinois], which was later declared a Superfund site [a toxic area needing cleanup] because of tons of PCBs dumped there, and wonder, usually in the most abstract and impersonal of ways, what effects the contaminants of that era had on me and my generation. Use of chlorinated compounds like DDT and PCBs peaked in the 1960s and tainted all our foods, even our mothers' breast milk, and children whose mothers ate a lot of PCB-tainted fish from Lake Michigan have lower IQs and worse memories, according to ten years of research conducted in Michigan. I also wonder, as only a mother could, whether my son suffered some slight neurological damage from the pesticides and other chemicals I was exposed to. He's healthy, he's smart. But could some neurotoxin explain why his handwriting is so sloppy and he has trouble tying his shoes? Absurd, you say? These worries, though, are the inevitable spinoff of this new generation of environmental science. These private musings have driven my desire to understand and explain to readers the risks of toxic chemicals, particularly to pregnant women and their newborns.

Until a few years ago, I felt reassured that the worst was over, that *Silent Spring* was so successful in its crusade against the most pervasive and persistent compounds that the book was no longer relevant. But I know now that other chemicals are simply taking their place. Compounds still widely used in household products, farms, and factories are building up in animal and human bodies at an extraordinary pace, and some seem to have effects similar to the PCBs, DDT, and others that were banned decades ago. We have simply exchanged one risk for another.

The question we face about toxic pollutants is no longer "Do we want to save the world?" but "How safe do we want to be?" In the twenty-first century, our Fable for Tomorrow is not some disaster we are trying to avert but a vague, incalculable, and potentially serious threat to our children's health. We must remind readers that most environmental health decisions aren't a question of good versus evil. They amount to a judgment call, a trade-off. "We stand now where two roads diverge," Carson wrote in the final chapter of *Silent Spring*. "The choice, after all, is ours to make."

# Silent Spring Exaggerated the Case Against Pesticides

*Ronald Bailey*

*Ronald Bailey is the science editor for* Reason, *a libertarian monthly magazine. His books include* Liberation Biology: The Scientific and Moral Case for the Biotech Revolution *and* Global Warming and Other Eco Myths: How the Environmental Movement Uses False Science to Scare Us to Death.

*In the following viewpoint, Bailey argues that Rachel Carson's book exaggerated its claims about the dark side of pesticides. Bailey points out that although chemicals such as DDT, Carson's chief target, clearly may be harmful to the environment, they also have many beneficial uses. Carson used misleading figures on the cancer rate in order to drive her argument against chemical agriculture, Bailey believes. The "great cancer scare" that Carson launched has long since been counteracted by subsequent scientific studies, according to Bailey. Even if Carson's concerns about the effects of pesticides were partly justified, Bailey suggests, and concludes that in light of the data from such studies, Carson's legacy is a troubling one, for billions of dollars have been wasted fighting imaginary hazards.*

The modern environmentalist movement was launched at the beginning of June 1962, when excerpts from what would become Rachel Carson's anti-chemical landmark *Silent Spring* were published in *The New Yorker*. "Without this book, the environmental movement might have been long delayed or never have developed at all," declared then-Vice President Albert Gore in his introduction to the 1994 edition. The foreword to the 25th anniversary edition accurately declared, "It

Ronald Bailey, "*Silent Spring* at 40: Rachel Carson's Classic is Not Aging Well," *Reason*, June 12, 2002. Ronald Bailey is science correspondent at *Reason* magazine and Reason.com, where this column first appeared in June 2002. Reproduced by permission.

led to environmental legislation at every level of government." In 1999 *Time* named Carson one of the "100 People of the Century." Seven years earlier, a panel of distinguished Americans had selected *Silent Spring* as the most influential book of the previous 50 years. When I went in search of a copy recently, several bookstore owners told me they didn't have any in stock because local high schools still assign the book and students had cleaned them out.

## DDT and the Rise of Chemical Agriculture

Carson worked for years at the U.S. Fish and Wildlife Service, eventually becoming the chief editor of that agency's publications. Carson achieved financial independence in the 1950s with the publication of her popular celebrations of marine ecosystems, *The Sea Around Us* and *The Edge of the Sea*. Rereading *Silent Spring* reminds one that the book's effectiveness was due mainly to Carson's passionate, poetic language describing the alleged horrors that modern synthetic chemicals visit upon defenseless nature and hapless humanity. Carson was moved to write *Silent Spring* by her increasing concern about the effects of pesticides on wildlife. Her chief villain was the pesticide DDT.

The 1950s saw the advent of an array of synthetic pesticides that were hailed as modern miracles in the war against pests and weeds. First and foremost of these chemicals was DDT. DDT's insecticidal properties were discovered in the late 1930s by Paul Muller, a chemist at the Swiss chemical firm J.R. Geigy. The American military started testing it in 1942, and soon the insecticide was being sprayed in war zones to protect American troops against insect-borne diseases such as typhus and malaria. In 1943 DDT famously stopped a typhus epidemic in Naples in its tracks shortly after the Allies invaded. DDT was hailed as the "wonder insecticide of World War II."

As soon as the war ended, American consumers and farmers quickly adopted the wonder insecticide, replacing the old-fashioned arsenic-based pesticides, which were truly nasty. Testing by the U.S. Public Health Service and the Food and Drug Administration's Division of Pharmacology found no serious human toxicity problems with DDT. Muller, DDT's inventor, was awarded the Nobel Prize in 1948.

DDT was soon widely deployed by public health officials, who banished malaria from the southern United States with its help. The World Health Organization credits DDT with saving 50 million to 100 million lives by preventing malaria. In 1943 Venezuela had 8,171,115 cases of malaria; by 1958, after the use of DDT, the number was down to 800. India, which had over 10 million cases of malaria in 1935, had 285,962 in 1969. In Italy the number of malaria cases dropped from 411,602 in 1945 to only 37 in 1968.

The tone of a *Scientific American* article by [chemist and nutritionist] Francis Joseph Weiss celebrating the advent of "Chemical Agriculture" was typical of much of the reporting in the early 1950s. "In 1820 about 72 per cent of the population worked in agriculture, the proportion in 1950 was only about 15 per cent," reported Weiss. "Chemical agriculture, still in its infancy, should eventually advance our agricultural efficiency at least as much as machines have in the past 150 years." This improvement in agricultural efficiency would happen because "farming is being revolutionized by new fertilizers, insecticides, fungicides, weed killers, leaf removers, soil conditioners, plant hormones, trace minerals, antibiotics and synthetic milk for pigs."

In 1952 insects, weeds, and disease cost farmers $13 billion in crops annually. Since gross annual agricultural output at that time totaled $31 billion, it was estimated that preventing this damage by using pesticides would boost food and fiber production by 42 percent. Agricultural productivity in the United States, spurred by improvements in farming practices and technologies, has continued its exponential increase. As a result, the percentage of Americans living and working on farms has dropped from 15 percent in 1950 to under 1.8 percent today.

## The Dark Side of DDT

But DDT and other pesticides had a dark side. They not only killed the pests at which they were aimed but often killed beneficial organisms as well. Carson, the passionate defender of wildlife, was determined to spotlight these harms. Memorably, she painted a scenario in which birds had all been poisoned by insecticides, resulting in a "silent spring" in which "no birds sing."

The scientific controversy over the effects of DDT on wildlife, especially birds, still vexes researchers. In the late 1960s, some researchers concluded that exposure to DDT caused eggshell thinning in some bird species, especially raptors such as eagles and peregrine falcons. Thinner shells meant fewer hatchlings and declining numbers. But researchers also found that other bird species, such as quail, pheasants, and chickens, were unaffected even by large doses of DDT. On June 14, 1972, 30 years ago this week, the EPA banned DDT despite considerable evidence of its safety offered in seven months of agency hearings. After listening to that testimony, the EPA's own administrative law judge declared, "DDT is not a carcinogenic hazard [a cancer-causing agent] to man. . . . DDT is not a mutagenic [an agent that causes mutations] or teratogenic [an agent that disturbs growth] hazard to man. . . . The use of DDT under the regulations involved here [does] not have a deleterious effect on freshwater fish, estuarine organisms, wild birds or other wildlife." Today environmental activists celebrate the EPA's DDT ban as their first great victory.

Carson argued that DDT and other pesticides were not only harming wildlife but killing people too. The 1958 passage by Congress of the Delaney Clause, which forbade the addition of any amount of chemicals suspected of causing cancer to food, likely focused Carson's attention on that disease.

For the previous half-century some researchers had been trying to prove that cancer was caused by chemical contaminants in the environment. Wilhelm Hueper, chief of environmental cancer research at the National Cancer Institute and one of the leading researchers in this area, became a major source for Carson. Hueper was so convinced that trace exposures to synthetic chemicals were a major cause of cancer in humans that he totally dismissed the notion that smoking cigarettes caused cancer. The assertion that pesticides were dangerous human carcinogens was a stroke of public relations genius. Even people who do not care much about wildlife care a lot about their own health and the health of their children.

## Carson's Role in the Cancer Scare

In 1955 the American Cancer Society predicted that "cancer will strike one in every four Americans rather than the present estimate of one in five." The ACS attributed the increase to "the growing number of older persons in the population." The ACS did note that the incidence of lung cancer was increasing very rapidly, rising in the previous two decades by more than 200 percent for women and by 600 percent for men. But the ACS also noted that lung cancer "is the only form of cancer which shows so definite a tendency." Seven years later, Rachel Carson would call her chapter on cancer "One in Four."

To bolster her case for the dangers of DDT, Carson improperly cited cases of acute exposures to the chemical as proof of its cancer-causing ability. For example, she told the story of a woman who sprayed DDT for spiders in her basement and died a month later of leukemia. In another case, a man sprayed his office for cockroaches and a few days later was diagnosed with aplastic anemia. Today cancer specialists would dismiss out of hand the implied claims that these patients' cancers could be traced to such specific pesticide exposures. The plain fact is that DDT has never been shown to be a human carcinogen even after four decades of intense scientific scrutiny.

Carson was also an effective popularizer of the idea that children were especially vulnerable to the carcinogenic effects of synthetic chemicals. "The situation with respect to children is even more deeply disturbing," she wrote. "A quarter century ago, cancer in children was considered a medical rarity. *Today, more American school children die of cancer than from any other disease* [her emphasis]." In support of this claim, Carson reported that "twelve per cent of all deaths in children between the ages of one and fourteen are caused by cancer."

Although it sounds alarming, Carson's statistic is essentially meaningless unless it's given some context, which she failed to supply. It turns out that the percentage of children dying of cancer was rising because other causes of death, such as infectious diseases, were drastically declining.

In fact, cancer rates in children have not increased, as they would have if Carson had been right that children were especially susceptible to the alleged health effects of modern chemicals. Just one rough comparison illustrates this point: In 1938 cancer killed 939 children under 14 years old out of a U.S. population of 130 million. In 1998, according to the National Cancer Institute, about 1,700 children died of cancer, out of a population of more than 280 million. In 1999 the NCI noted that "over the past 20 years, there has been relatively little change in the incidence of children diagnosed with all forms of cancer; from 13 cases per 100,000 children in 1974 to 13.2 per 100,000 children in 1995."

Clearly, if cancer incidence isn't going up, modern chemicals can't be a big factor in cancer. But this simple point is lost on Carson's heirs in the environmental movement, who base their careers on pursuing phantom risks. The truth is that both cancer mortality and incidence rates have been declining for about a decade, mostly because of a decrease in the number of cigarette smokers.

## The Trouble with *Silent Spring*

The Great Cancer Scare launched by Carson, and perpetuated by her environmentalist disciples ever since, should have been put to rest by a definitive 1996 report from the National Academy of Sciences [NAS], *Carcinogens and Anticarcinogens in the Human Diet*. The NAS concluded that levels of both synthetic and natural carcinogens are "so low that they are unlikely to pose an appreciable cancer risk." Worse yet from the point of view of anti-chemical crusaders, the NAS added that Mother Nature's own chemicals probably cause more cancer than anything mankind has dreamed up: "Natural components of the diet may prove to be of greater concern than synthetic components with respect to cancer risk."

Meanwhile, Carson's disciples have managed to persuade many poor countries to stop using DDT against mosquitoes. The result has been an enormous increase in the number of people dying of malaria each year. Today malaria infects between 300 million and 500 million people annually, killing as many as 2.7 million of them. Anti-DDT activists who tried to have the new U.N. treaty on persistent organic pollutants totally ban DDT have stepped back recently from their ideological campaign, conceding that poor countries should be able to use DDT to control malaria-carrying mosquitoes.

So 40 years after the publication of *Silent Spring*, the legacy of Rachel Carson is more troubling than her admirers will acknowledge. The book did point to problems that had not been adequately addressed, such as the effects of DDT on some wildlife. And given the state of the science at the time she wrote, one might even make the case that Carson's concerns about the effects of synthetic chemicals on human health were not completely unwarranted. Along with other researchers, she was simply ignorant of the facts. But after four decades in which tens of billions of dollars have been wasted chasing imaginary risks without measurably improving American health, her intellectual descendants don't have the same excuse.

# Silent Spring's Critics Distort Carson's Case

**Brian Bethune**

*Brian Bethune is a senior writer for* Maclean's, *a Canadian weekly magazine.*

*In the following viewpoint, published on the centenary of Carson's birth in 2007, Bethune looks at the still raging controversy over* Silent Spring. *Though Carson is still lionized among environmentalists for her groundbreaking work on chemical pollution of the environment, Bethune reports, a growing number of antagonists have sought to poison her reputation. Chief among their contentions, Bethune writes, is that* Silent Spring's *supposed advocacy for the elimination of pesticides has led to the deaths of millions of Africans from malaria. But, as Bethune points out,* Silent Spring *never counseled readers to eliminate all pesticide use. Bethune explains that the book argues instead that the excessive use of chemical agriculture needed oversight. Moreover, he adds, DDT was not the malarial panacea her critics believe it to be, because DDT does not work as well in tropical climates, and mosquitoes soon developed resistance to it. Thus, Bethune contends, those who demonize Carson and her book are both misreading* Silent Spring *and distorting reality.*

In 1962, *Silent Spring* sparked a violent summer storm in the U.S., as Rachel Carson's beautifully written assault on the effects of widespread chemical spraying raced up the bestseller lists. Carson, already ill with the breast cancer that would kill her two years later, faced a furious chemical-industry counter-campaign, complete with lawsuits and the sexist insults so casually tossed about in her time. The FBI investigated her as a

Brian Bethune, "Was Rachel Carson Wrong?" *Maclean's*, June 4, 2007, pp. 42–43.

potential Communist agent out to disrupt the national food chain. A former government marine biologist, Carson had no financial backing or institutional support, but she did have credibility as a well-known and gifted writer on natural history. Public opinion, already alarmed by spraying programs, swung decisively to her side.

In the year of her centenary [2007]—Carson was born May 27, 1907—it's difficult to overestimate her significance. *Silent Spring* is one of the most influential books of the 20th century, and its author the founding mother of modern environmentalism. In America, pesticide use, particularly DDT, was severely curtailed by her efforts, while the Environmental Protection Agency (1970) and the Endangered Species Act (1973) followed in Carson's wake as surely as dying birds trail an oil spill. David Suzuki, Canada's own ecological icon, once said, "Rachel Carson essentially directed my life." An elementary school, a bridge, and a Maryland state park all bear her name. Her birthplace in Springdale, Penn., is a national historic site. For biographer Linda Lear, that's about the least her country owes Carson "for showing what a single individual could accomplish by speaking out, and for warning us about the arrogance with which we approach the natural world."

## Carson's Critics

But, for a vocal minority, it's Carson's very reputation—her status as a saint in what they dismiss as a secular religion—that makes her legacy poisonous. Websites and op-ed pages accuse her of a straight-line responsibility for the deaths of millions of Third World malaria and yellow fever victims since the 1970s. That's when, the critics say, a Carson-inspired ban on DDT destroyed humanity's best defence against the disease-bearing mosquitoes that kill more than a million people every year. Having used DDT in the First World long enough to wipe out malaria there, they add, eco-imperialists now prevent its use anywhere, saving African birds at the cost of African children, malaria's prime victims.

The attacks are more notable for their venom than their attention to detail. Consider Dennis Avery's mid-April posting on the website of the American Conservative Union Foundation. Avery, formerly a senior analyst for the State Department and currently at the Hudson Institute, mistakenly marked Carson's birthday on April 12. He blames her for "at least" 30 million deaths—meaning everyone who has died of malaria or yellow fever in the last 40 years. That figure, he goes on to claim, is "five times as many as Hitler killed in his concentration death camps, albeit inadvertently"—a statement that manages to be at once vicious, factually wrong (about four million Nazi victims died in the death camps) and syntactically absurd (assuming Avery means Carson was the accidental killer, not Hitler).

But being sloppy and prone to bizarre Hitler analogies are par for the course in media fulminations [rants]. Style doesn't necessarily mean Avery and like-minded souls such as Steven Milloy of JunkScience.com are wrong. The story they tell would be a grotesquely ironic instance of the law of unintended consequences at work, were it true. But it's not. For all the vitriol—Milloy thinks Carson's name should be stripped from public property—it's astonishing how weak the case against Carson is. For one thing, critics completely ignore the situation in her day.

## Defending *Silent Spring*

In a just-released book of tributes to Carson, Edward O. Wilson, probably the most distinguished environmental scientist in American history, describes the temper of the times. Living better chemically—and atomically—barely captures it. Wilson sat on a U.S. National Research Council committee that evaluated a proposal to create a new, parallel Panama Canal by a series of precisely timed nuclear explosions. (They voted it down.)

One project that did get off the drawing board was the fire-ant eradication program of 1958, discussed at length in *Silent Spring* and vividly recalled by Wilson who, as a bug-mad 13-year-old Boy Scout in 1942, was the first person to record the arrival of the invasive South American species at the docks near his Mobile, Ala., home. In what Wilson calls the "Vietnam of Entomology," the U.S. Agriculture Department sprayed a million acres with powerful insecticides. Wildlife and livestock developed fatal nervous disorders, while bird and beneficial insect populations were decimated. The effect on human health was never assessed. The fire ants, who bear the Latin name *invicta* ("unconquered") for good reason, easily survived the carpet bombing.

When Carson's critics argue—although not without dispute—that 30 years of research have shown DDT to be less toxic for humans than most environmental contaminants, it's worth remembering that no one knew that in 1962. In that year of DDT's peak usage, 80 million kg were sprayed across the U.S., without any idea of its long-term effects.

As for Carson's responsibility for malarial deaths, the word of environmentalists is far from the only thing curtailing DDT use in the Third World. In the glory days of the Chemical Era, the World Health Organization [WHO] commenced a program in 1955 to eradicate malaria worldwide via DDT. At first it was highly successful (reducing mortality rates from 192 per 100,000 to seven per 100,000), but resistance soon emerged in insect populations. Widespread agricultural use of DDT—just like the agricultural use of antibiotics—sped up the development of resistant strains, inflicting lasting harm on health care. But even before resistance took hold, DDT was less effective in tropical regions than in North America and Europe because of inefficient infrastructures and the continuous life cycle of mosquitoes there. The WHO program, in fact, was never applied in sub-Saharan Africa for those reasons, and that is why mortality rates there never fell to the same extent as elsewhere, and why Africa remains the epicentre of the epidemic. The WHO abandoned its ambitious goal of eradication in 1969, and now focuses its attention on controlling the disease.

## Carson Criticized Arrogance, Not Judicious Pesticide Use

DDT, sprayed in judicious amounts on interior walls, remains the best malaria control known. Carson, in fact, would probably not have stood with those environmentalists opposed to any use of DDT. *Silent Spring* called not for a ban on pesticide use, but for increased study, a precise weighing of costs and benefits and, above all, humility in the face of what we still don't know about the natural order. For Rachel Carson, arrogance—corporate, governmental, scientific or environmental—was always the enemy.

# Carson Won a Battle but Lost the War over Environmental Policy

*Colin Tudge*

*Colin Tudge is a British broadcaster and science writer. His books include* Consider the Birds: How They Live and Why They Matter *and* The Secret Life of Trees.

*In the following viewpoint, Tudge writes about the changes that Rachel Carson's "great green book" brought about worldwide, including its effect on Tudge's own England. But Tudge wonders if the battles that Carson won were of limited effectiveness, for, as he asserts, even while presidents and prime ministers took notice and responded to the charges Carson made in* Silent Spring, *the ultimate achievements of her work were limited. Today, Tudge observes, despite the global response to* Silent Spring, *genetically modified organisms have created some of the same problems that Carson wrote about, and humans continue to harm the environment in new, creative ways.*

Did Rachel Carson win her battle with the pesticide companies, which threatened effectively to eliminate North America's wildlife, and after that, the world's? Or have her victories been illusory? She dented the confidence of the big commercial battalions; she caused governments to quell their zeal, at least up to a point, which they do not do lightly; she alerted people at large to the rising threat, which is the *sine qua non* [indispensable quality]; and she showed, vitally, that individuals can make a difference. But the birds she sought to protect are dying anyway—not from toxins, but just as surely through starvation; and the agricultural strategy that produced the pesticide excesses of the 1950s and 1960s continues to dominate world agriculture, with protest reduced to noises off and regarded as an irritant (not least by [English prime minister] Tony Blair's government). All in all, Carson started the modern environment movement, for which she deserves the gratitude of all humanity. But her campaign cannot be won in a single battle. If we are truly to reconcile productive agriculture with wildlife then we have to dig very deep indeed, to the roots of our economy and morality, and then, in effect, start again.

## Always a Writer

Carson belongs to that long and honourable tradition of great naturalists-cum [as]-writers that runs from [Englishmen] John Ray and Gilbert White, through Charles Darwin, Alfred Russel Wallace and Thomas Huxley, to John Maynard Smith, Ed Wilson and Bill Hamilton. She was born on 27 May 1907 on her parents' estate by the beautiful Allegheny River in Philadelphia. She communed with the wild creatures, attended the Presbyterian church and published her first article at the age of ten in the *St Nicholas Magazine*, the *Blue Peter* [a British children's television show] of its day. As she commented in 1954, "I can remember no time . . . when I didn't assume I was going to be a writer"; and biology is, inter alia [among other things], a literary pursuit.

All was not as it might seem, however. Her family was horribly strapped for cash (her father was a not very successful salesman), the nearby town of Springdale stood between power stations and stank of glue, while her reckless siblings married badly but frequently and hung round her like desperate ghosts throughout her life. Yet—largely through enormous parental sacrifice—she was thoroughly educated as a biologist, first at the genteel Pennsylvania College for Women, then at the Marine Biological Laboratory at Woods Hole and at Johns Hopkins. Finally she entered the US Fish and Wildlife Service as a biologist and editor and so, between 1941 and 1951, completed her careful and lyrical maritime trilogy: *Under the Sea Wing*, *The Sea Around Us* and *The Edge of the Sea*. But somewhere along the way she developed cancer and had to endure the rigours of the heroic but crude radiations and chemotherapies of the 1950s and 1960s. She died in 1964—her brother grotesquely arriving at her funeral to organise a grand but vulgar service which overturned her request for a quiet and dignified passing.

## *Silent Spring's* Greater Meaning

Hers would have been a good, hard but unremembered life, straight from [American author] Louisa May Alcott—except that in the 1950s, Carson saw that the wild creatures she had known in her childhood and studied professionally were now dying: not covertly growing rarer but slaughtered in all too horribly visible heaps. The general cause was familiar enough from her childhood: pollution. More specifically, however, the birds were killed by pesticides, most of which belonged either to the organochlorine family, which began in the 19th century with DDT (discovered in 1874, though not used as a pesticide until 1939) and later gave rise to dieldrin, aldrin and endrin; or to the organophosphates, which had been developed initially as nerve gases for chemical warfare and now provided malathion and parathion. These were all sprayed by the tonne on serious pests and trivial irritants alike. Although already terminally ill and not by nature combative, Carson set to work on *Silent Spring*. It was published in 1962 and, says her Penguin editor and erstwhile [former] biographer Linda Lear, it has changed the course of history as surely as [Karl Marx's] *Das Kapital* or [Charles Darwin's] The *Origin of Species*.

Carson shows in *Silent Spring* how easy it is to be fooled by pesticides—and how blithely the scientists fell into the many traps. Thus, the residues may remain for months or years in the soil—sometimes changing chemically yet remaining toxic, so that aldrin, for example, degrades into dieldrin. In this way, a scientist who tests for aldrin residues would find none—and then conclude wrongly that the danger was ephemeral. Intake of residues may be small, but they accumulate in fat and build up through the food chain: so a worm picks up a small amount, and the songbird that eats it absorbs what is in the worm and stores it, and the hawk that eats the songbird accumulates lethal quantities (or enough to render it effectively sterile). No one knew in detail the effects of residues, or how different types might enhance the toxicity of others. Scientists did not anticipate the rapid evolution of pesticide resistance. All in all, as Carson pointed out, it is both in practice and in theory impossible to anticipate all the tricks that nature might pull. Yet scientists *qua* employers and civil servants happily asserted that the dangers were negligible, and farmers and various environmental agencies took their word for it. It beggars belief.

Carson was subjected to the full repertoire of dirty tricks. Excellent professional biologist though she was, she lacked a Ph.D. (she couldn't afford the extra study) and so was dubbed an "amateur". Worse, she was a woman—and as the then famous critic William B. Bean waggishly remarked, "trying to win an argument with a woman . . . cannot be done". But [US president] John F. Kennedy, fresh from the Cuban missile crisis, ordered an inquiry which led at last to legislation. There are still abuses, of course, but at least it was reluctantly accepted in principle even in the land of the free that essential freedoms do not include the right to scatter serious toxins like snow.

## Not Enough Has Changed

This was victory of a kind, but the economic imperatives that prompted the pesticide mania still predominate. Western governments take it to be self-evident that agriculture must be driven primarily by profit, and that whatever is profitable and

*A protestor at a testing ground for genetically modified (GM) crops in Warwickshire, England, 2002. Environmentalists are concerned that GM crops will disrupt the balance of sensitive ecosystems around the world. © Sion Touhig/Getty Images.*

done with good intentions cannot be bad. Protests in the name of the environment, rural employment, human happiness, animal welfare or aesthetics are shuffled to one side. In Carson's day, the ancient, flowery meadows were sprayed with pesticides and so the birds died. Today—as [British soap opera] *The Archers'* excellent agricultural adviser Graham Harvey is wont to point out—the meadows have been replaced with monocultural rye grass leys where the insects can find nothing to eat, so the birds are dying in any case since they, too, must starve.

More specifically, Carson wrote in *Silent Spring*: "It is not my contention that chemical pesticides must never be used. I do contend that we have put poisonous and biologically potent chemicals indiscriminately into the hands of persons largely or wholly ignorant of their potentials for harm." Make genetically modified organisms the subject of those sentences, and what's changed?

# Social Issues
in Literature

# CHAPTER 3

# Contemporary
Perspectives on
the Environment

# Modern Capitalism Causes Needless Waste of Natural Resources

*David R. Loy*

*David R. Loy is Best Professor of Ethics Religion and Society at Xavier University in Cincinnati, Ohio. He is the author of* A Buddhist History of the West *and* The Great Awakening: a Buddhist Social Theory.

*In the following viewpoint, Loy contends that economics and ecology are inseparable, so governments must alter their economic systems to save the planet from a catastrophic environmental future. At present, he maintains, the capitalist system that dominates the world depletes natural resources to create wealth. But Loy argues that the wealth created is not real: money is an artificial creation of civilizations that has no inherent value. Thus humans are sacrificing the earth's resources for nothing. Loy promotes the principles of Buddhism as guideposts toward living a better, more benevolent and valuable life by respecting the natural world.*

"The American way of life is not negotiable."

So declared President George H. W. Bush at the 1992 Earth Summit in Rio de Janeiro [Brazil]. It was his response to what everyone else there had realized: that the earth's ecology is endangered and "that nothing less than a transformation of our attitude and behavior would bring about the necessary changes" to protect it, according to Maurice Strong, the secretary-general of the conference.

David R. Loy, "The Nonduality of Ecology and Economy," *Tikkun: A Bimonthly Interfaith Critique of Politics, Culture, & Society*, September–October 2009, pp. 31–32, 84–85. Reprinted with permission from *Tikkun: A Bimonthly Interfaith Critique of Politics, Culture, & Society*.

A ten-year follow-up to the Earth Summit was held in 2002, but [Bush's son] President George W. Bush did not bother to attend. When his White House press secretary Ari Fleischer was asked whether the new president would encourage Americans to reduce consumption in order to reduce pollution, he said no: "The American way of life is a blessed one."

## Valuable Time Lost

What happened during those ten years? Unfortunately, not very much. After the Earth Summit it seemed like the world had finally awakened to the eco-crisis, and for a couple of years I noticed that almost every media report on the oil industry referred to global warming. And then . . . the world seemed to fall asleep again. The environmental crisis was not really forgotten, but the linkage between ecology and economy was de-emphasized—and so very little was achieved, because not much can be achieved without addressing their interconnectedness.

Why did so little happen during that decade? It's only a guess, but I suspect that two different reactions reinforced each other. Corporations—especially oil companies—realized that the new green movement was a threat to their profit margins, and rather than restructure they decided to fight, with a massive advertising and propaganda campaign designed to muddle the issue by denying climate change. (Jim Hansen, who is the head of NASA and a globally respected climatologist, has called their misinformation campaigns "crimes against humanity.") At the same time, consumers began to realize the same thing—that the eco-crisis is a serious challenge to consumerism—and rather than change the "blessed American way of life" it was easier to ignore the problem. After all, the experts disagree, don't they? The result was mass denial. At some level of consciousness, many if not most people were aware that the environment was deteriorating, but that didn't have much effect on our day-to-day lives. As the economy boomed, most of us consumed more than ever.

As a result, much valuable time has been lost, and the need for drastic change has become even more urgent. Yet that will not happen until we realize the nonduality of ecology and economy. Although most people still see the issue as merely a technological problem to be solved by lowering carbon emissions, atmospheric carbon is only the visible tip of a much more ominous iceberg. According to the United Nations Environment Program, one in four mammalian species, one in eight bird species, one in three amphibian species, and 70 percent of all the world's plant species are now endangered. Global warming, along with deforestation, agriculture, and urbanization, could drive half of all species on earth to extinction by 2100, according to eminent biologists such as Edward O. Wilson of Harvard University. Ninety percent of all large fish species have been driven toward extermination. Depleted water tables are becoming a global problem, and since 1950 the world has lost about 30 percent of its arable land and soil fertility.

## The End of Business as Usual

Most of us are familiar with these grim facts, but too often such statistics remain abstract and disconnected from our lives. We overlook the institutions that mediate between the biosphere and our own patterns of consumption: the world's globalizing economic system, which today is seven times as large as it was in 1950.

The fact that 20 percent of the Amazon rainforest ("the lungs of the earth") has been cut down in recent decades needs to be connected with our "need" for more soybeans to feed the cattle and pigs who provide our beef and pork. The fact that almost all large fish species are endangered is a consequence of the high-tech ship-factories that trawl the oceans with enormous drift nets. Most fresh water is used for agriculture and manufacturing; vast amounts of topsoil are lost because of industrial farming. And so forth.

It would be a serious mistake to blame everything on capitalism. Most of us (at least in the "developed world") have benefited much from the affluence provided by its innovative dynamism. The old Soviet Union was not capitalist, it was a classic example of "command socialism"—and its ecological record was perhaps the worst of all developed nations. What capitalism and state socialism have in common is a preoccupation with industrialization, which has accelerated and taken on a life of its own.

Today, however, socialism is more or less dead, and globalizing capitalism is the only game in town. Our collective relationship to the biosphere and its ecosystems is largely mediated by what corporations do, and what they do is largely determined by what is most profitable—quite apart from the ecological consequences, which still tend to be ignored or "externalized" when possible.

The result is an unsustainable economic system supported by a deluded worldview. All the world's economies are wholly owned subsidiaries of the earth's biosphere, but we still have great difficulty understanding what that implies. Yes, it does mean the end of business-as-usual. It means the greatest possible challenge to consumer capitalism, whose corporations must either mutate into something very different, or be replaced altogether. And this is a transformation that Buddhists should embrace and encourage, because it is also implied by the teachings of the Buddha.

## Better Software for the Economy

The news media have been telling us that the financial crisis—which is far from over—is due to the excessive greed of Wall Street speculators and the unbridled spending of Main Street borrowers. Yet the problem goes much deeper, and our predicament is much worse. Greed is not a virus that has infected the economic hard drive; it has become the software that runs our economy.

Buddhism does not say much about evil itself, but it emphasizes the three roots of evil: greed, ill will, and delusion. The basic problem with our present economic system is that it institutionalizes the first of those roots. As [Professor] George Lakoff put it on May 22 in the *Huffington Post*, "the economic and ecological meltdowns have the same cause: the unregulated free market and the idea that greed is good and that the natural world is a resource for short-term private enrichment. The result has been deadly, toxic assets, and a toxic atmosphere." Two sides of the same coin.

Greed also takes two forms, according to our means. As [Austrian philosopher] Ivan Mich argued, "In a consumer society there are two kinds of slaves: the prisoners of addiction and the prisoners of envy."

The Buddha's first noble truth identifies dukkha (dissatisfaction) as inherent to the human condition. It is the nature of an unawakened mind to be bothered by something. We usually experience this as the feeling that "something is wrong with me." Our economic system (which includes the media mega-corporations that make their profit from advertising) takes advantage of this and conditions us to understand our sense of lack as "I don't have enough . . ."—especially not enough things and not enough money. The consequence is that we always want ("need") more. This individual lack is institutionalized into a collective craving that can never be satisfied. Investors seek increasing returns in the form of dividends and higher share prices. This puts pressure on business executives, who must think this way if they hope to rise to the top. This general expectation translates into an impersonal but constant demand for ever more profit and growth, which requires ever more production-and-consumption, and ever more sophisticated advertising to make us want things that often didn't even exist last year.

Here's one way to point out the basic difficulty: Capitalism is about using capital (money for investment) to create more capital. Since the goal is to end up with more money, everything else becomes a means to that end. "Everything else" in this case includes Mother Earth ("resources"), human life ("labor"), and society itself, which must continually adapt to the changing requirements of the economy.

## Converting the Whole Biosphere to Nothing

The ultimate irony is that money in itself is literally worthless: whether pieces of paper or numbers in bank accounts, money has value only because it is our socially agreed-upon medium of exchange. A $100 bill is just a piece of paper. We can't eat it, drink it, ride on it, etc. We forget that money is a social construct—a kind of group fantasy. The anthropologist Weston LaBarre called it a psychosis that has become normal, "an institutionalized dream that everyone is having at once."

This dream can become a nightmare. Psychologically, the danger is that means and ends become reversed, so the means of life becomes the goal. The [German] philosopher [Arthur] Schopenhauer called money "abstract happiness"—that is, not genuine happiness but something that now represents it in our culture. Another way to say it is that money becomes "frozen desire": not desire for anything in particular but a symbol for the satisfaction of desire in general. And what does the Buddha say about desire? Frozen or not, it remains the root cause of suffering.

Collectively, this means that what motivates our economic system is the drive to use anything and everything (now called "natural resources," including "human resources") to create something that is really nothing. We don't usually notice the absurdity of this because we are preoccupied with the more and more that the system produces. The fact that so many of us already have more than we need is addressed by manipulating our awareness, in increasingly sophisticated ways, so that we always want something else that we don't yet have. It's always the next (fill in the blank) that will satisfy us.

[Swiss author] Max Frisch said technology is the knack of arranging the world so that we don't have to experience it. That's why modern technologies fit so well with consumer capitalism, which works to transform the whole biosphere into consumer goods. Together they are making Mother Earth into a gigantic Wal-Mart.

This system is unsustainable because it involves a growth obsession that, left to itself, will not cease until the whole of the biosphere has been converted into profit—which, of course, will then be useless. Capitalism made more sense a couple of centuries ago, when the earth seemed infinite and capital was relatively scarce. Today the obvious metaphor is cancer on a planetary scale. Cells become cancerous when they mutate into uncontrolled growth and spread throughout the body to disrupt its healthy functioning. Unfortunately, that is not a bad description of our collective situation now.

Ultimately, does it come down to a choice between our present economic/financial system and the survival of the biosphere? Our current system is doomed no matter what, in the same way that a cancer is always doomed: if it's successful enough to kill its host, it kills itself. If the biosphere gets sick, we get sick. When ecological systems collapse, so will human civilization as we know it.

Despite what President George H. W. Bush and his son both declared, the "blessed American way of life" is negotiable—or it becomes a suicide pact.

This means that the financial meltdown is actually a wonderful opportunity to address a much deeper problem. No one should make light of the economic pain that we can expect to continue and deepen over the next few years. Many—perhaps most—people are also disgusted with the present system, and are becoming more open to possible alternatives.

Such a crisis would be a terrible thing to waste because this sort of opportunity does not happen very often. There is no better time to address the fundamental challenge of our times: the intimate relationship between an out-of-control, self-destructive economic system and the ecological crisis.

## Reason for Hope

No other nation is in a position to begin reforming that relationship, which is why [President Barack] Obama's leadership on this issue is so important to the whole world. Admittedly, this is an extraordinary challenge. According to the Center for Public Integrity, in the last year more than 770 corporations and interest groups have hired an estimated 2,340 lobbyists to influence federal policy on climate change. That number is more than three times what it was only five years ago, and it means that Washington now has more than four climate lobbyists for every member of congress. The center also estimates that lobbying expenditures on climate change topped $90 million last year, a figure that will no doubt be much higher this year.

That puts the onus on the rest of us to emphasize the nonduality between ecology and economy. So far, at least, Obama's economic appointments have not been encouraging. Some of the people most responsible for the financial crisis have been appointed to fix it. No wonder the only solution they can think of is to try to patch up the present system. But they only represent a much bigger problem: the people who benefit the most from our present economic system—and who therefore have the least incentive to change it—are the ones who control it and (through their lobbyists) control much of the political process as well. As [American comedian] Will Rogers put it some eighty years ago, we (still) have "the best Congress money can buy."

Nevertheless, Obama has given us reasons to hope that he might rise to the occasion and grow to meet the challenge. Yet even with the best will in the world, this is not something Obama (or anyone else) can do by himself. Very little will happen without broad public pressure, based on a new understanding of our perilous situation. This does not require a specifically Buddhist movement, but there is need for a Buddhist voice in such a movement, to emphasize our nonduality with the earth, and the karmic [relating to one's actions and conduct] effects of greed and delusion, both individual and institutionalized.

# Pesticides Are Still Poisoning the Planet

*Christopher D. Cook*

*Christopher D. Cook is an award-winning investigative journalist whose work appears in* Mother Jones, Harper's, *the* Nation, *and elsewhere. He is author of* Diet for a Dead Planet: How the Food Industry Is Killing Us.

*In the following viewpoint, Cook writes that despite the warnings of* Silent Spring *almost fifty years ago, more pesticides and herbicides than ever are imperiling life on Earth. Such toxins, he declares, pollute groundwater, lakes, rivers and streams, the air, and even large bodies of water such as the Gulf of Mexico. Cook points out that measurable concentrations of poisonous chemicals are found in all of these environments, and yet despite the warnings of ecologists the agricultural industry is addicted to petrochemicals. It doesn't have to be this way, Cook stresses. He maintains that there are, as Rachel Carson once wrote, numerous natural alternatives to using pesticides. But he concludes that today's food industry has become dependent on using chemical means to produce huge surpluses of food, thus keeping wholesale prices down and increasing profits for food processors, fast food chains and supermarkets.*

When Rachel Carson's *Silent Spring* was published in 1962, the American pesticide business was in full postwar bloom. These "elixirs of death," descended from World War II chemical warfare experiments, were suddenly ubiquitous—growing fivefold from 124 million pounds in 1947, to 637 million by 1960. Roughly 60 percent of these synthetic potions, some 375 million pounds, were applied on food. Toxic

Christopher D. Cook, "The Spraying of America," *Earth Island Journal*, vol. 20, no. 1, 2005, pp. 34–38. Reproduced by permission.

residues from pesticides were found everywhere: in water systems; in animals, including the "vast majority of human beings"; even in that most sacred nectar, mother's milk. That now-infamous poison, DDT, was "so universally used that in most minds the product takes on the harmless aspect of the familiar."

## More Pesticides Than Ever

Fast-forward 40 years: President George W. Bush, campaigning for a second term, eases restrictions on pesticide use by farmers and homeowners. In a move cheered by agribusiness and pesticide producers, the Bush administration enables the Environmental Protection Agency—often criticized for issuing permissive pesticide standards—to approve pesticides on its own, without consulting other federal agencies about effects on endangered species. Court-ordered "no-spray zones," established along rivers to protect salmon and other fish, could soon be rolled back. Using toxins that may imperil life just got easier.

The food industry benefits from a decided hush when it comes to today's silent spring. With concerns about genetically modified foods capturing the headlines—as well as the attentions of most food-industry critics today—the grave ecological effects of pesticides have been relegated to the back burner.

After decades of activism and success banning "dirty dozen" pesticides such as DDT and chlordane, we are told a cleaner future lies ahead. In the brave new high-tech world of bio-engineered crops, like the [biotechnology firm] Monsanto potato that secretes its own pesticide, it seems we needn't worry ourselves about poisoned farmworkers, pesticide drift, and children munching on toxic apples. Genetically modified crops are, according to USDA and corporate biotech officials, helping to cleanse the environment by reducing pesticides. As Bush's agriculture secretary Ann Veneman told a UN Food and Agriculture Organization conference, biotechnology promises to "make agriculture more environmentally sustainable."

The facts clearly refute the happy claims of Veneman and the politically connected GMO [genetically modified organism] business: American industrial agriculture today dumps close to one billion pounds of pesticides on food crops, producing a truly toxic harvest.

Despite public assurances of a kinder, gentler agriculture, the biotech and pesticide businesses march hand-in-hand, two sides of the same corporate coin. The industry's most prominent product, Monsanto's "Roundup Ready" soybean, was designed to withstand intensive spraying, thus expanding sales of the firm's highly popular—and highly toxic—herbicide, Roundup. Since the 1996 introduction of Roundup Ready, the use of glyphosate, a key Roundup ingredient that studies have linked to [the blood cancer disease] non-Hodgkin's lymphoma, has risen.

Roughly 85 percent of all cropland in America relies on herbicides—a business which will remain stable as long as agribusiness fights off new pesticide bans and maintains the myth that biotech is eliminating toxins in the fields.

Since the publication of *Silent Spring*, the amount of pesticides applied to our food has more than doubled. In 1997, according to industry figures, US growers poured more than 985 million pounds of pesticides onto their crops. The US accounts for more than one third of the $33.5 billion in global pesticide sales, the vast majority for farming. That's an $11 billion business interest for the petrochemical and biotech industries to protect.

They've protected it well, perpetually—though not always successfully—fighting and delaying new regulations to limit toxins in the fields. After a modest decline in the 1980s, the amount of pesticides used each year has increased by more than 100 million pounds since 1991. At the same time, there's been a dramatic increase in costs borne by farmers, whose spending on herbicides has more than doubled since 1980. Each year, over 100 million pounds of highly toxic active ingredients from pesticides are released into the environment in California alone.

## Polluting the Groundwater

If it were merely a matter of waiting for Rachel Carson's DDT ghosts of the 1960s to fade away, we might one day be in the clear. Rivers, lakes, fish, and birds might, over time, cleanse themselves of these toxins. But agriculture's chemicals continue to flood our water and air with contamination. What is particularly startling is the degree to which pesticides have spread throughout the entire environment. One might lament the plight of poisoned farmworkers or the effects of pesticides on farming communities and consign them to the realm of regrettable problems over which one has little control. While few would openly counsel reckless disregard for the health of farmworkers and their families—who pay a very high price for our pesticide-based food system—it is all too easy to ignore and forget.

But according to a 1998 analysis by the California Public Interest Research Group, nearly four million Californians live within half a mile of heavy applications of pesticides, a third of which are "designated by state or federal regulatory agencies as carcinogens, reproductive toxins or acute nerve poisons."

Spring, if not silent, is no doubt quieter. Every year agricultural pesticides alone kill an estimated 67 million birds. An array of disturbing side effects is in store for those lucky enough to survive a sublethal dose, including "increased susceptibility to predation, decreased disease resistance, lack of interest in mating and defending territory, and abandonment of nestlings," according to a 1999 report by Californians for Pesticide Reform and the Pesticide Action Network.

A key indicator of today's pesticide pollution epidemic lies underground, in the hidden waters that ultimately percolate up into rivers, lakes, and wells. Groundwater is the source of 50 percent of America's drinking water, and it is intimately interconnected with surface water.

Since the late 1970s, studies have found more than 139 different pesticide residues in groundwater in the US, most frequently in corn- and soybean-growing regions. One study of a Nebraska aquifer found numerous pesticides at "lifetime health advisory" levels. All of the samples contained atrazine, the most commonly-used pesticide applied to America's cornfields. In Iowa, toxic chemicals are found in roughly half of the groundwater.

Even closer to home were the findings of a 1992 national pesticide survey by the EPA, which discovered that ten percent of community wells "contained detectable levels of one or more pesticides." Well water samples gathered by the California Department of Pesticide Regulation show residues of 16 active ingredients and breakdown products from agricultural pesticides.

Groundwater pesticide presence, though, pales in comparison with the chemicals' prevalence in surface rivers and streams. In California, state regulators detected pesticides in 95 of 100 locations in the Central Valley. More than half of these sites exceeded safe levels for aquatic life and drinking water consumption. In Kentucky, where farmers annually apply roughly 4.5 million pounds of the top five herbicides, these chemicals showed up routinely in rivers. A two-year study by the state Department of Environmental Protection discovered atrazine and metolachlor, both used heavily on corn, in a full 100 percent of the 26 river sites they examined; another chemical, simazine, was found 91 percent of the time.

## Polluting the Streams, Rivers and Lakes

The spread of these toxins is a serious matter affecting both environmental and public health. Atrazine, found widely in drinking water across the Midwest and detectable on many foods, is a "possible human carcinogen," according to the EPA. Studies suggest it may cause ovarian cancer.

Nationwide reports are equally troubling and reveal a bath of chemicals harmful to fish and the broader freshwater ecosystem. In a ten-year study examining thousands of streams across the country, the US Geological Survey [USGS] traced the proliferation of numerous agricultural pesticides: atrazine was in 90 percent of the streams; deethylatrazine and metolachlor were in 82 percent of all samples, others were detected at least 40 percent of the time. Still more disquieting was a 1999 USGS finding of an average of 20 pesticides, mostly agricultural, at each river or stream tested. Chemical concentrations of some compounds were frequently found to exceed allowable levels in drinking water, and one or more standards for protecting aquatic life were exceeded in 39 of 58 sites.

In studies conducted over the past 30 years, nearly half of all pesticides targeted for research were found in stream sediment, and some 64 percent in edible fish, mollusks, and other aquatic life.

More and more, scientists are observing important changes in hormones and reproductive systems among fish and other waterborne creatures exposed to pesticides. One study of sex hormones in carp revealed that the ratio of estrogen to testosterone in both males and females was "lower at sites with more pesticides."

Pesticides may also be a factor behind rising numbers of frog deformities, such as extra or missing limbs. In a 2002 study published in the *Proceedings of the National Academy of Sciences*, biologist Joseph Kiesecker compared frogs in several Pennsylvania ponds, with and without pesticide runoff. The rate of misshapen frogs was neatly four times higher in the ponds with pesticides.

Environmentalists and scientists are not the only ones complaining. Fishing enthusiasts are angry about the poisoning of their prey. Randy Fry of the Recreational Fishing Alliance of Northern California has written that pesticide pollution "seriously impacts the estuary's food-web and thereby limits the productivity of Central Valley populations of salmon, steelhead, striped bass, and sturgeon while increasing the pollutants carried by these fish." Fry has noted declines in fisheries throughout the Valley.

## Polluting the Air

Perhaps the greatest—yet most elusive—measure of pesticides long reach is their presence in the air we breathe. "Nearly every pesticide that has been investigated has been detected in air, rain, snow, or fog across the nation at different times of year," says the US Geological Survey. Given just a lazy breeze, toxins can migrate for miles. A seemingly innocuous spraying or fumigation of a rural farm field can let pesticides drift through air currents for hours, even days, ending up as residue in nearby towns, ruining organic crops downwind and further polluting waterways. Diazinon, a highly volatile agent sprayed widely on nuts and stone fruit, actually increases its drift concentrations as time passes, the greatest amount of drift showing up two to three days after spraying. Although levels generally diminish, pesticide drift can last for weeks, and sometimes months after application.

The epicenter for the pesticide drift problem, particularly its human effects, is California, where decades of suburban sprawl—and intensely consolidated agriculture—have wedged burgeoning population centers up against farms. Blending agriculture with suburbs would seem a fine rural-urban complement but for the rampant use and drift of pesticides, which are exceedingly toxic, even at low levels, for children "Pesticides in air are often invisible and odorless, but like secondhand cigarette smoke, inhaling even small amounts over time can lead to serious health problems, especially for children," reports Susan Kegley, staff scientist for the Pesticide Action Network.

More than 90 percent of pesticides used in California (including non-agricultural pesticides) are likely to drift, and roughly a third of those are highly toxic to humans, according to a 2003 study by Californians for Pesticide Reform. Samples of two pesticides, chlorpyrifos and metam sodium, taken near sprayed fields, produced residues that were, respectively, some 184 and 111 times the acute exposure standards set by government for a one-year-old child.

## Pollution in the Gulf of Mexico

The Gulf of Mexico is afflicted with a "dead zone" stretching across several thousand square miles along the Louisiana-Texas coast. A massive algae bloom feasts on a steady diet of nitrogen and other nutrients flowing downstream from the Mississippi River. In summer, when the river's flow peaks, the bloom spreads and chokes the Gulf's northern coasts, cutting off oxygen that supports sea life. In 1999 the zone ballooned to nearly 12,500 square miles—the size of New Jersey. The depleted water near the bottom of the Gulf contains less than two parts per million of dissolved oxygen, not enough to sustain fish or bottom-dwelling life.

One of the chief contributors to this dead zone is American agriculture and its countless tributaries of petroleum-based fertilizers, pesticides, and animal feces overflowing from giant factory farms. The Mississippi River Basin, which drains an area representing about 41 percent of the contiguous US, is home to the majority of the nation's agricultural chemicals. About seven million metric tons of nitrogen in commercial fertilizers are applied in the Basin each year, and the annual load of nitrates poured from the Mississippi River into the Gulf has tripled since the late 1950s, when pesticides and synthetic fertilizers began to dominate the agricultural scene. Another key ingredient is on the rise: billions of tons of factory-farm animal waste, overloaded with nitrogen and other potentially damaging nutrients.

In 1999, when Congress, the EPA and environmental groups pressed for cuts in farm pollution to clean up the Gulf of Mexico, some agricultural trade groups raised the specter of farm closures and diminished food production. "Crop yields in the Midwest could shrink if federal regulators try to reduce use of fertilizers to cut pollution in the Mississippi River and in the Gulf of Mexico," the Associated Press reported, summing up the agribusiness argument. Asking farmers to reduce fertilizers would be "basically asking them to go out of business," said Cliff Snyder, representing the Potash and Phosphate Institute. "It would have a significant economic impact if producers were required to reduce nutrient input . . . at a time when the farm economy is dismal."

Despite the economic trap, some forward-looking farmers are contemplating ways to either use less synthetic fertilizer, which itself is quite costly, or at least drain their fields away from rivers, perhaps into wetlands that could use the nitrogen.

## Fertilizing Sterility

Beyond the Gulf case, chemical fertilizers—laden with nitrogen, ammonia, and phosphorus, as well as trace toxic metals like cadmium—are a serious environmental problem. Overshadowed in the public mind by pesticides, synthetic chemical fertilizers severely deplete and erode soil and drain toxic nutrients into the water supply. They have become a perilous crutch—with over 14 million tons applied annually, seven tons per square mile in the upper Midwest—injecting excessive nutrients into the ground, and ironically, robbing soil of its fertility. A 1984 World Bank report concluded that American agriculture's growing reliance on synthetic fertilizers "has allowed farmers to abandon practices—such as crop rotation and the incorporation of plant and animal wastes into the soil—which had previously maintained soil fertility."

## The Petrochemical Addiction

Why has pesticide use increased even in this time of growing ecological awareness? In *Living Downstream*, scientist-author Sandra Steingraber describes the political economy that has driven agriculture into a self-feeding cycle of poison. First, the arrival of synthetic pesticides following World War II reduced labor on the farm. Simultaneously, profits per acre began to shrivel. "Both these changes pressed farmers into managing more acres to earn a living for their families." Bigger farms, and federal subsidies promoting mono-crop agriculture, "further increased the need for chemicals to control pests. And the use of these chemicals themselves set the stage for additional ecological changes that only more chemicals could offset."

The decline of crop rotation in favor of monocropping— the planting of the same crop year after year—enables insects to adapt and recover, continuing the upward chemical spiral. Through Darwinian natural selection, the strongest few insects able to resist insecticides "become the progenitors of the next generation as their more chemically sensitive compatriots are killed off," explains Steingraber. Thus pesticides ultimately create insects that are less susceptible to them. During the postwar pesticide revolution between 1950 and 1990, the number of insect species resistant to pesticides mushroomed from fewer than 20 to more than 500. In roughly the same period, the amount of crops lost due to insect damage doubled.

## Alternative Measures

It doesn't have to be this way. Agriculture can be prolific and efficient without pesticides. The miraculous march of American agriculture toward unparalleled productivity long before the postwar pesticide revolution is a compelling testimonial to the possibilities of organic farming. Before agribusiness' petrochemical addiction, farmers used crop rotation and diversified agriculture to replenish soils and keep pests on the run. Crop diversity supplied sustenance for farm families and livestock and a natural insurance policy against pest outbreaks or weather disasters.

While many so-called "conventional" growers have bravely made the transition into organics—itself a lengthy and costly process for which there is virtually no government support—the wider food economy and the profits of agribusiness rely on farmers' continued deployment of chemical warfare in the fields. The near-perennial American surplus fueled by petro chemicals keeps farm crops cheap, not so much for consumers as for the intermediary complex of food processors, fast-food chains, and supermarkets.

Back in the days of *Silent Spring*, the US had for years been stockpiling food, requiring ever-larger subsidy payments and growing pressures on exports and food aid. As Carson remarked then, "We are told that the enormous and expanding use of pesticides is necessary to maintain farm production." Yet, she said—noting that American taxpayers were paying more than $1 billion a year for this surplus food storage—"Is our real problem not one of over-production?" Excess supply is primarily a problem for farmers, both here and abroad, who are forced by price-depressing surpluses to "get big or get out." For the petrochemical industry and its close partner, the biotech business, today's economy of surplus production and exports, and of a mono-crop industrial agriculture stripped of its natural sustainability, is not a problem at all. Except that they, too—and their children—must inhabit a poisoned world.

# Environmentalists Devalue Human Life

*Wesley J. Smith*

*Wesley J. Smith is a senior fellow in human rights and bioethics at the Discovery Institute, a conservative think tank, and author of* A Rat Is a Pig Is a Dog Is a Boy: The Human Cost of the Animal Rights Movement.

*In the following viewpoint, Smith attacks the environmental movement, claiming a new ecocide initiative is further proof that environments value nature more than they respect humanity. The ecocide movement, according to Smith, claims that crimes against the environment by businesses, corporations, and countries are tantamount to war crimes. Such thinking, Smith believes, is subversive to progress, commerce, and even the sanctity of human life. A believer in the concept of human exceptionalism, Smith contends that people have the right to use nature as they see fit and that extreme environmentalism is too dangerous to be ignored.*

Environmentalism is growing increasingly antihuman. Having left Teddy Roosevelt-style conservation and Earth Day consciousness-raising behind, the cutting edge of the movement is pursuing utopian "save the planet" agendas while angrily castigating mankind for supposedly sucking the life out of Gaia.

## An Antihuman Philosophy

Such environmental misanthropy used to be confined to the fringe. For more than three decades proponents of Deep Ecology [movement that considers environmental concerns as im-

Wesley J. Smith, "Ecocide: a Crime Against Peace? Just When You Thought the Environmental Movement Couldn't Get Worse," *The Weekly Standard*, vol. 15, no. 32, May 10, 2010. Reproduced by permission of *The Weekly Standard*.

portant as human ones] have urged "environmental egalitarianism" and radical depopulation to beat back the human "invasion" of nature. Alas, in recent years such advocacy moved from the flanks toward the center of environmentalism—to the point that some of the world's leading global warming warriors now echo the radical depopulation agenda as an urgent imperative to protect polar bears and keep glaciers from melting.

Global warming alarmists and other über-environmentalists also promote anti-prosperity, seeking to convince developed nations to constrict their economies drastically and redistribute much of their remaining wealth to developing countries as an inducement for them to remain mired in low emissions poverty. The advocates of this view see economic decline as a goal. Thus, in the run up to the failed Copenhagen global warming summit, *New Yorker* writer David Owen asserted that "the world's principal source of man-made greenhouse gases has always been prosperity." He warned darkly that the recent "environmental benefits of economic decline, though real, are fragile, because they are vulnerable to intervention by governments."

The antihuman and anti-prosperity impulses in environmentalism have also led to granting human-type rights to the birds and the bees and the flowers and the trees. Under the influence of American environmental radicals, the leftist government of Ecuador won ratification for a new constitution that formalized the "rights of nature" along with those of humans. Several municipalities in the United States have taken the same route. In 2007, Tamaqua, Pennsylvania, enacted an ordinance purporting to strip sludge-and-dredge corporations of all constitutional rights within the town—an empty gesture given the town had no such authority—while granting rights to "nature" enforceable in court by any resident.

Allowing radical environmentalists to enforce the putative rights of nature could certainly stifle development. But it might not eliminate it. To do that, punitive action is required. Indeed, how better to push us back toward a hunter/gatherer (or just plain gatherer) ideal than to criminalize large-scale economic development?

That's precisely the goal of This Is Ecocide, a new environmental campaign mat seeks to outlaw serious pollution as an international "crime against peace," akin to war crimes or genocide. Anyone indicted for ecocide would find himself in the dock at the International Criminal Court alongside such alleged mass murderers as Serbia's [former President] Radovan Karadzic and Liberia's [former president] Charles Taylor.

## Ecocide Defined

But what is ecocide, precisely? Practically any business activity that environmentalists loathe, from large scale resource development to nonrenewable energy generation, along with any accidental ecological disaster would potentially qualify as a crime against peace. As envisioned by ecocide's rising star, Polly Higgins, who recently addressed the United Nations promoting a Universal Declaration of Planetary Rights, the This Is Ecocide website states:

> Ecocide is the extensive destruction, damage to or loss of ecosystem(s) of a given territory, whether by human agency or other causes, to such an extent that peaceful enjoyment by the inhabitants of that territory has been severely diminished.

Note that "peaceful enjoyment by the inhabitants" is a very broad term, intended to include everything from grass, fish, and insects to mice, snakes, and people. And diminishment of "peaceful enjoyment" would not require actual pollution, but could mean a declining supply of forage or a loss of foliage caused by almost any use of the land, perhaps even simple urban growth.

Not only that, but the crime of ecocide would be so encompassing that any company involved in large scale resource development would almost certainly commit it. Again, from the website:

- Ecocide arises out of human intervention. Heavy extraction, toxic dumping, release of pollutants can all result in ecocide.

- Ecocide is a crime of consequence, e.g., where an energy company procures its energy by extracting fossil fuels, as opposed to creation from renewable energy, that would result in ecocide.

- Ecocide is not a crime of intent. The intention is rarely to render damage on a given territory, more often it is an outcome of another primary (economic or war) activity.

It is worth noting that the website does not cite deliberate ecological despoliation among its examples of ecocide; it makes no mention, for instance, of Saddam Hussein's releasing oil into the Persian Gulf and setting oil wells aflame during the first Gulf war. Its prime target is resource development, such as oil extraction from the Alberta tar sands and large mining projects. Under this view, the *Exxon Valdez* accident could be elevated from a civil wrong justly requiring Exxon to pay billions in damages to a crime requiring the jailing of the company's CEO for life. There need not even be harm to any living organism: The proliferation of space junk is listed as ecocide.

One need not read between the lines to perceive that the real culprit isn't pollution as much as it is human prosperity created by industrialization. Thus, declaring the need to "abolish planetary slavery," the YouTube video "Ecocide: A Crime Against Peace" states:

We have come to accept that extraction of natural resources is normal. Just because it is normal does not mean that it is right. Two hundred years ago companies plundered for profit. Then it was called colonization. Today it is called business.

Back then, extraction often led to conflict. Sometimes it led to war. Now a century of "resource wars" is predicted. The battle to control oil and water has already started. Now natural resources are becoming the reason for war. Unless we change. Do you see what is happening here?

PowerPoint style, the screen then slowly rolls out the phrase "Extraction = Ecocide > Resource Depletion > War," which melts into the summary statement "Ecocide > War."

## A Dangerous Concept

The concept of ecocide is subversive on several levels. First, equating resource extraction and/or pollution with genocide trivializes true evils such as the slaughter in Rwanda, the killing fields of Cambodia, the [Soviet] gulags, and the death camps, while elevating undefined environmental systems to the moral status of human populations. Even more elementary is the fact that ecocide's promoters want to destroy prosperity by criminalizing necessary economic activities.

The cliché that green is the new red is proving all too true. Increasingly, environmental activism promotes utopian hysteria, undermines human exceptionalism by personalizing nature, and exhibits disturbing totalitarian symptoms. Ecocide fits squarely within this emerging zeitgeist. Tempted as we may be to laugh it off, we should instead recognize it as a potential threat to our collective future.

# The 2010 Gulf Oil Spill Provides Lessons About Preventing Future Disasters

*Douglas N. Rader*

*Douglas N. Rader is chief ocean scientist of the Environmental Defense Fund's North Carolina office in Raleigh.*

*In the following essay Rader suggests that while the 2010 Deepwater Horizon oil spill in the Gulf of Mexico was a disaster of unprecedented proportion, perhaps some good can be taken from the experience. America can learn many important lessons about the environment from the mistakes that were made both leading up to and following the explosion and subsequent spill, Rader asserts. First, he argues, the industrial and government overseers of the oil industry were woefully unprepared to anticipate and correct a disaster of this magnitude. Second, he points out, though oil industry insiders have worked hard to convince the public that the spill did minimal damage, the facts reveal that the environmental toll on the Gulf is catastrophic and must not be understated. Rader concludes by offering numerous corrective steps that may be taken to minimize similar future events and correct current problems.*

Pundits have been speculating that the unprecedented British Petroleum [BP] oil disaster in the Gulf of Mexico [in 2010] will become a "game changer," in the same way that the now-infamous 1969 fire on the Cuyahoga River [in Northeast Ohio] spurred a generation of environmentalism, stimulated the passage of the National Environmental Policy Act. Clean

Douglas N. Rader, "Perhaps the 'Gusher in the Gulf' Was Not for Naught," *USA Today Magazine*, September 2010, pp. 14–16. Reproduced by permission.

Water Act, and other pillars of modern environmental law, and led to the creation of the Environmental Protection Agency under Pres. Richard Nixon—a man not known as terribly green.

It remains to be seen whether the events in the Gulf will lead to breakthrough momentum to rebuild the wetlands of coastal Louisiana, protect disadvantaged communities against rising seas and intensifying storms, inject momentum into still-struggling climate legislation, or fuel the fires for a green energy portfolio for the U.S.'s future.

## Lessons to Be Learned

Nonetheless, there are essential lessons to be drawn from the "Gusher in the Gulf," so that the prodigious ecological damage and the economic, social, and health injuries to coastal residents from four states can be assessed fairly and offset, and measures taken to reduce the risk of repetition while the nation seeks a more secure energy future.

As public attention wanders back to [singer] Lady Gaga and [actor] Leo DiCaprio, it is essential to "out" the red herrings that have been perpetrated in the name of continuing dependence on fossil fuels. Perhaps the most insidious patent medicine being sold these days is the suggestion that the BP oil disaster happened only because of the confluence of extremely unlikely—nearly impossible—factors, and that there is next to no chance it will happen again.

While the falseness of this it-cannot-happen-here mantra seems obvious, there is important texture that bears examination. In 2009-10, I co-chaired North Carolina's Legislative Subcommittee on Offshore Energy Exploration, finalizing our report April 13, one week before the *Deepwater Horizon* [the well that caused the oil spill in 2010] shattered the confident fairy tale of U.S. Outer Continental Shelf invincibility. Our subcommittee heard repeated, confident assurances by oil industry specialists as well as Federal and state regulators that a major blowout like the 1979 *Ixtoc I* in the Bay of Campeche [in the Gulf of Mexico] or the 2009 oil disaster in the East Timor Sea [near Australia] simply could not occur here, and there was no point reexamining that prospect. After all, the track record of oil industry operations in U.S. waters—and of the agency formerly known as the Minerals Management Service (MMS) since it was created after the 1969 Santa Barbara [California] blowout—nearly was spotless. The testimony to this obscure state panel is important because it reflects the hubris of the pro-drilling partnership and, from a regional perspective, because North Carolina's offshore waters figure prominently in every "drill baby drill" map, whether from Congress or the president, despite massive economic and ecological liabilities.

## The Ecological Toll

Undoubtedly, the most disappointing aspect of this disaster is just how unprepared the industry and government overseers were for a worst-case accident. The real shocker was not that this occurred in U.S. waters, but that it took so long to happen on the MMS watch. After all, thousands of widgets and hundreds of people are engaged in each complex drilling and production exercise, and errors do occur. Similarly, it should be no surprise that it was the Gulf's fragile ecology and tightly linked human communities that drew the short straw, with the now-venerable decision to "do" oil whole hog. The reverberations of that decision pervade the Gulf's history, society, culture, politics, economics, and environment. Just to be clear: it remains inevitable that another serious blowout will occur if the U.S. persists in depending on deepwater drilling for oil.

Second, industry apologists are working hard to convince the public that the blowout in the Gulf is not all that serious, that a bunch of leftwing loons exaggerated the risks and the tales of damage done. Besides, they maintain. Mother Nature will heal the Gulf. Trust us, they insist, the fish, shrimp, and crabs all are safe to eat.

This set of arguments is just plain wrong. The ever-expanding litany of the dead—nearly 70 marine mammals, almost 800 sea turtles, and more than 3,500 sea birds—certainly is understated and a tiny fraction of the untold number of deaths of animals of all types that has been and will be caused by oil-based pollution. After all, out of the total of roughly 220,000,000 gallons spewed from the broken well during the 87 worst days (if the BP "guestimates" turn out to be anywhere close to correct), less than 50,000,000 were collected or burned, leaving around 175,000,000 gallons to be accounted for.

Perhaps the greatest death toll occurred near the sea surface, a seething profusion of life, including countless tiny plants and animals, including babies of larger life forms. The top few millimeters host extraordinarily important processes that regulate not only gas exchange with the atmosphere, but many other foundational ecological relationships. In the Gulf, the vast majority of seafood species spawn offshore, producing buoyant babies that float with the surface currents back towards the marshes where their nurseries lie. A loop current oscillates through the Gulf, carrying baby reef fish, lobsters, and other reef biota [plant and animal life] from spawning grounds—often far upcurrent in the Caribbean—toward adult habitats downstream, in the Gulf and beyond.

The only thing that limited the damage to some degree was the chance formation of a large eddy on June 1 that cut itself off from the main loop current, and persisted for the next six weeks, sucking in oil and protecting the loop current riders. Had that event not occurred right when it did—just as the leading edge of the oil was entering the rapid delivery system—not only would there have been significant oil on downcurrent coral reefs, mangrove swamps, seagrass beds, and beaches from Cuba to Florida and beyond, many more baby animals would have died.

In addition, the Gulf ecosystem and its human communities are linked tightly to those nearshore nurseries in the surf and marshes—now oiled over more than 600 linear miles. Besides the resident oysters, clams, and fishes being in trouble, the crabs, shrimp, and marine fish that use them are as well. These marshes sustain the massively valuable shrimp and oyster fisheries, and the less-well-known, but largest, Gulf fishery for menhaden. Menhaden are filter feeders, quite fragile, extremely vulnerable to oil, and key prey for many other species of fish, birds, and mammals. Gulf marshes and beaches will continue to regenerate oil—and the toxins it contains—for years.

To make things worse, the oil originated from nearly 5,000 feet down, rising slowly through the entire ocean from bottom to top, moving with the currents, and being sorted and winnowed as some toxicants dissolved or separated and began traveling separately at many different depths, leading to the notorious undersea plumes of oil-based pollution that took three expeditions worth of proof before government officials believed. Just because the pollution is not oil per se (in its recognizable black, gloppy form) does not make the impacts any less real or important.

## Death in the Gulf

Think of it: 175,000,000 gallons of residual oil means as much as 50,000,000 gallons of extremely toxic lighter-weight poisons such as benzene, toluene, ethyl benzene, and xylene (materials normally evaporated in a surface spill) being processed and taken by biota, and entering food-webs of the Gulf. That would he considered a major pollution event by any standard.

Animals in other strata also were poisoned by oil-based pollution. On the bottom—right under the main oil plume, and potentially bathed in undersea poisons—lie ancient deep-water coral reefs, some millions of years old, containing species never before seen. Moreover, the middle depths of the sea sustain a huge profusion of life so dense that sonar beams from the surface bounce back from it, creating a "deep scattering layer" that provides essential prey for diving predators of many types, from great whales and dolphins to sharks, tuna, and billfish.

Add 1,800,000 gallons of dispersants, injected into the oil geyser or on the surface—a major toxic spill in its own right—and you have a real problem. Bottom application, especially, likely will turn out to be a bad idea: spreading out and breaking up the rising oil pollution, making it more transportable, exposing a wider area and a greater array of biota, including those that inhabit bottom waters, mid-level depths, and surface layers. Moreover, dispersing oil actively inhibits collection.

EPA press releases based on scanty data from toxicity trials of dispersants alone conducted on standard laboratory species simply do not apply to highly susceptible life stages of pure marine organisms from many depths. Relatively little scientific work has been done on the toxicity of the oil-dispersant combinations. For at least some compounds, biological uptake of toxicants is facilitated by dispersants. My guess is that the bottom line ultimately will be that dispersant use ought to be employed only when collection is not possible, and maybe not even then. This "toxic ignorance" is unacceptable for a major weapon in off-the-shelf oil spill contingency plans, a centerpiece of the current and inadequate oil spill response arsenal.

While much has been made (justifiably) of the burning of sea turtles, total deaths probably are far worse since all surface collection—whether by skimming, vacuuming, or burning—kills animals of all sizes. A fair assessment of trade-offs in total deaths among these approaches will be required to make objective judgments about optimal approaches to future worst cases. Calculating the extent of total damage in this broad and interconnected mosaic will be quite challenging. For many elements, incomplete baseline data exists. For most, there is inadequate science to be able to specify with any degree of cer-

*Crews attempt to subdue the blaze caused by an explosion on the Deepwater Horizon oil rig on April 20, 2010. The explosion produced a massive oil spill that experts estimate released between 100 and 300 million gallons of crude oil into the Gulf of Mexico.* © AP Images/ Gerald Herbert.

tainty the damage that has been—and is being—done. Even tracking the transport and fate of the hundreds of chemicals in oil through die Gulf will be a daunting task.

The reports by fishermen of large numbers of dead sea cucumbers—virtually ignored in the press—illustrate the point. What killed them on the bottom? Did they die from oil, from dispersants, or from lack of oxygen (when oil was consumed by bacteria)? What other undocumented mass mortalities occurred? No models yet exist to make sense of the extra oxygen demand the blowout has exerted, contributing to already low oxygen levels—more evidence of lack of preparedness for worst-case events.

## An Unprecedented Spill

Seafood testing protocols also are not up to the task of tracking the movement of toxicants from oil traveling independently through the complex Gulf trophic [pertaining to the food chain] web. Oil spills typically require testing only for polycyclic aromatic hydrocarbons (PAHs), which, while quite toxic and persistent, exist in low concentrations in oil. Rarely, if ever, is significant testing conducted for benzene (a known human carcinogen) or toluene (a powerful reproductive toxin) in fish. It is unclear whether the "sniff" test is adequate.

There simply is no precedent for a scientific and management challenge like this—not the *Amoco Cadiz* nor the *Exxon Valdez* [large oil spills]. Indeed, even *Ixtoc I* is not especially useful in that regard. The disaster occurred in a distant cul-de-sac of the Bahia de Campeche—far from the sensitive environments that were later assessed—at a shallow depth, allowing a significant proportion of the total pollution to be evaporated or burned. Oil drifted all the way across the Gulf before it hit the 162 miles of Texas beaches that widely have been reported to have been damaged for only a few years. The vast majority of the more serious impacts from *Ixtoc* never was characterized, since no applicable baselines existed, and follow-up studies were minimal. Even so, significant oil still can be found among the mangroves nearby.

## Key Takeaways for Future Practice

Nonetheless, there are important lessons to be learned from the *Deepwater Horizon* disaster:

- The existing oil and gas infrastructure in the Gulf must be updated and remediated. There are 4,000 wells and more than 30,000 linear miles of pipelines. A complete and objective inventory is required to catch other problems that MMS missed, and to upgrade the general expectations for day-to-day operation of this massive subsea industry.

- New wells in all depths must be subjected to heightened performance expectations and lower allowable risk. While improved safety standards cannot absolutely prevent a recurrence, they are an obvious first step, and a good start. The Obama Administration's "time out" to examine the level of upgrading that is needed makes tremendous sense, and the grossly premature calls for return to business as usual represent an unacceptable financial risk.

- The expectation that increasingly deepwater exploration in the Gulf and elsewhere in U.S. waters must occur as part of the nation's energy strategy needs reevaluation. Deepwater fundamentally is risky, especially when the target is oil. To open vast new areas of coastal waters to drilling—including many areas where drilling would put at risk sensitive environments, and the economies that rely upon clean beaches and healthy fish populations—must be reconsidered in light of the BP disaster.

- The nation's need for natural gas to balance the overall energy budget as our society transitions off of the oil habit should cause our leaders to reconsider the current approach to Outer Continental Shelf leasing, where production of liquid petroleum— tremendously riskier in environmental terms— inevitably is co-mingled with production of natural gas. It well may be that a safer, and saner, strategy would be to drill only (or principally) for natural gas, while leaving oil in the ground as a resource of greater prospective value for other uses. Even flat-out production in U.S. waters cannot reduce the price for oil at the pump significantly, as it is a global commodity.

- All future drilling must be preceded by fair and objective worst-case environmental and social impact analysis, and accompanied by resources adequate to respond when those worst-case events occur. Deep-water wells will require tremendously greater response capacity.

- Oil spill contingency plans must be upgraded into the 21st century, with adequate investment in the science needed to make judgments about the tradeoffs involved in various response mechanisms, with improved resources for collection.

- Investments must be expanded in basic science related to the structure and function of susceptible ecosystems. At present, even guessing the bottom-line of cascading impacts on seafood species is daunting. Factoring implications of a shifted ecosystem into goal-setting for fisheries and protected species management will require a significant recommitment of resources.

- A high-level national science oversight panel must be created—perhaps in the president's Office of Science and Technology Policy—to ensure fair and accurate assessment of impacts across the spectrum, and to evaluate potential response mechanisms.

- Natural resource damage assessments must be upgraded to account accurately for all types of damage done to oceanic ecosystems, not just sea turtles, sea birds, and marine mammals. Under current approaches, there are no baselines, and thus no way to count (much less value) many of the damaged elements.

- A national commitment is needed to begin restoring the wetlands of the lower Mississippi Valley and the delta as a core need for a vibrant Gulf. Perhaps a greater challenge than even the Everglades, the development of sediment budgets and delivery strategies adequate to keep ahead of rising seas and local subsidence in the face of intensifying storms will require a decades-long national commitment. If the nation expects to continue to use the Gulf as a key energy source, we all must share in the associated price.

- Investments must be required from BP to mitigate key ecosystem damage. Wherever possible, optimal active interventions should be identified that have the best net impact on population condition for damaged species, based on the best available science.

- The people of the Gulf must be made whole. Their culture and livelihoods intimately and inextricably are tied to that body of water's health. Response and restoration workers must be compensated fairly for the risks they took. Their health, and that of the more generally exposed population, must be watched to ensure that whatever secondary health problems develop are taken care of by BP.

- Fishermen and other natural resource users must be compensated for lost income, not only associated with the closures, but for future losses as consumers worry about the safety of Gulf seafood. BP should pay for an expanded seafood safely program to ensure that Gulf seafood is in fact safe, and to educate consumers about that fact.

- Sustainable fishery programs of the type pioneered with the Gulf red snapper and reef fish should be expanded to reduce risk.

This oil disaster creates an opportunity for us as a nation to take responsibility for the decisions made in our name, over decades, to exploit the Gulf of Mexico as a central energy hub. The environmental, economic, and social impacts from the blowout will persist for years, if not decades. The degree to which we step forward, learn its lessons, and build from them a grander future will reflect on our society and our generation.

# Environmentalists Are the Enemy of Progress and Happiness

*James Delingpole*

*James Delingpole is a columnist and novelist. He has published several novels and two political books,* How to Be Right: The Essential Guide to Making Lefty Liberals History *and* Welcome to Obamaland: I Have Seen Your Future and It Doesn't Work. *He writes for the* Times *(London), the* Daily Telegraph, *and the* Spectator.

*In the following essay, Delingpole writes of his disdain for environmentalists. His dislike of "greens" is not based on simple prejudice against those who defend the environment, he says. Instead, he considers environmentalists to be dangerous—the real threat to those who enjoy the bounty of Mother Nature. Delingpole writes that if environmentalists are wrong about global warming, then their dire predictions are causing humanity to waste billions of dollars as well as having a negative impact on the quality of contemporary life. He maintains that climate change may be a natural occurrence and suggests that readers visit a selection of anti-environmental/conservative websites. Finally, Delingpole argues that environmentalist alarmists continually simplify complex situations in order to fit their own presuppositions.*

If only you could have seen the gratitude in my guinea pigs' eyes just now. At least I think it was gratitude. It's hard to be totally sure with those blank, dead, black staring eyes which, let's be honest, aren't noticeably more intelligent or expressive than a (very small) great white shark's. Even so, if Pickles

James Delingpole, "I Don't Bait Greens Only for Fun. I Do It Because They're Public Enemy Number One," *Spectator*, May 16, 2009, p. 29. Reproduced by permission.

Deathclaw and Lily Scampers [names of the guinea pigs] could speak, I like to think that what they would have said is this: 'Thank you, human. You are so kind and generous and nurturing. Every day come rain or shine you sweep our cage of poo, you transport us to our outdoor play run, feed us fresh titbits—sometimes delicious broccoli stalks, sometimes apple, sometimes fresh dandelion leaves which you have personally harvested—and seem to mind not one jot that we are actually pretty crap animals with scratchy, panic-stricken claws who show you no sign of affection whatsoever.'

If Nature—Ma Gaia as I sometimes call her because we are on such friendly, intimate terms—were to speak, I'm sure her report would be similarly rosy. 'Oh James,' she'd say. 'Dear, delightful, caring James. I did so appreciate the way you picked up all those horrid takeaway burger packs you found blowing round the pavement the other day. And your compost is coming on a treat, especially when you pee on it in that wholesome organic manner of which I so heartily approve. And I do like the way you're bringing up your children to share your love of slowworms and wild raspberries and Cocky Olly in the bracken. And well done on your campaign against wind farms: I bloody hate them too . . .'

## Public Enemy Number One

I mention all this lest some of you think that I am the embodiment of pure Gaiaraping evil. Maybe you'll have chanced upon jottings in which I have been less than respectful towards [former US vice president] Al Gore, [English writer and environmentalist] George Monbiot and the NASA scientist [and climatologist who warned of global warming] Dr James Hansen. Perhaps you'll have heard how I gave up recycling for Lent and found the penance so bracing I've decided to carry on till next Easter at the very earliest. Maybe you've caught me on talk radio pooh-poohing 'cap-and-trade' [an economic means to control pollution] or promising that if I sell enough copies of [Delingpole's book] *Welcome To Obamaland* I'll buy a 4x4 and run over a baby polar bear. 'Monster!' you may have decided. 'Heretic! Climate-change denier!'

Obviously there's a part of me that kind of enjoys this. As Americans love Coca-Cola and Islamists love death, so I love baiting greens and liberals and most especially liberal greens. But I don't do it just for fun, you know. In fact I don't even do it mainly for fun. The reason I rail so often against so many tenets of the green faith—from biofuels to carbon trading to the ludicrous attempts to get polar bears designated as an endangered species—is because I sincerely believe they are among the greatest current threats to the advancement of humankind. Yes, that's right: greens aren't the solution. They're public enemy number one.

Whenever my green friends hear me say such things—the nice Germans down the road who give us lift-shares in their electric car, say; Ralphie in Dorset [England] who's doing an MA [master's degree] studying Boris's [London mayor Boris Johnson] green policies—their assumption is that I'm just saying these things out of a sort of attention-seeker's Tourette's. 'You're turning into a shock jock!' they say. Or: 'Well I suppose this is what you do when you have a blog.' Here is what's so terrifying about the modern green movement: its complete refusal to accept that anyone who disagrees with it can be anything other than wilfully perverse, certifiably insane or secretly in the pay of Big Oil.

## What If Environmentalists Are Wrong?

This is true within the mainstream media too. Of all the different editors I write for, I would say that no more than 10 per cent would commission a piece in which I expressed even in passing the view that the man-made-global-warming theory is bunk and that climate change is nothing to worry about. Check out all the soft features in any newspaper. They were all commissioned by editors on the same middle-class ecoguilttrip: consumption is naughty, GM [automaker General Motors] is dangerous, organic is close to godliness, non-local produce is sinful produce, wind farms are actually rather striking and if they ruin every last square acre of unspoilt British upland, well, maybe that's just the price we'll have to pay—a bit like all those lovely old railings we had to melt down to win the last war.

But what if they're wrong? What if climate change is normal? What if the new hair-shirt chic is holding back economic recovery? What about the Kenyan greenbean growers—don't they deserve to make a living too? What if the billions and billions of pounds being stolen from our wallets by our governments to 'combat climate change' are being squandered to no useful purpose? What if instead of alleviating the problem, misguided eco-zealots are actually making things worse?

That's what I believe, anyway, and if there were space I'd be more than happy to explain why in lavish detail using all sorts of highly convincing evidence provided by top-notch scientists. Unfortunately, there isn't, so you'll have to go somewhere like www.ClimateDepot.com, or the hilarious Planet Gore at *National Review Online* or the *Watts Up With That* blog for your ammo.

My purpose here is not to convince any green waverers of the justice of my cause, merely to point up the quite nauseating arrogance and bullying self-righteousness with which the modern green movement cleaves to its ideological position. Indeed, it doesn't even think of its ideological position as an ideological position any more, but as a scientific truth so comprehensively proven that there is no longer need for any debate.

## Environmentalists Simplify Complex Issues

Hence the snotty dismissiveness with which they wave away our arguments. In their Manichean [dualistic] *weltanschauung* [worldview] the world now divides into two categories: on the one hand, caring, nurturing, sensitive, intelligent eco-types who understand the threat of global warming and want to make the planet a lovelier place; on the other, morally purblind, selfish, ugly, greedy deniers who can't even pass sea otters at play without thinking how much more entertaining they'd look drenched in tanker spillage.

I venture to suggest that the issues are rather more complex than that; that the vast majority of so-called "deniers" are motivated by a love of the planet every bit as intense as that of the "warmists". It's just that our love is maybe tempered with a touch more rationalism, that's all.

We look at electric cars and go: OK fine, but where does that electricity come from? We're told Tuvalu Polynesian Island nation is sinking and go: yeah, very worrying—except it's not. We're told temperatures will rise inexorably with carbon emissions and go: so how come we've just had three years of global cooling? We're told to heed scientists like NASA's Dr Hansen—only to discover that in the 1970s he was predicting an imminent ice age. We're told that plonking lots of vast, white, heavily subsidised, bird-chewing, subsonic-humming, light-stealing turbines on top of an unspoilt British landscape is just what we need to save the environment, and we go: now wait just a second, there's something here that doesn't quite ring true.

# DDT Should Be a Last Resort in Fighting Malaria

*NewsRx Health Editors*

NewsRx Health *is a publisher that creates and distributes medical and health-related articles.*

*In the following viewpoint, the editors of* NewsRx Health *review the current controversy over spraying DDT inside homes and buildings in Africa to prevent malaria. While DDT is commonly known to curb this deadly disease, the viewpoint author points out that the effects of spraying the carcinogenic chemical in high doses have never been thoroughly investigated. Instead, the viewpoint illustrates, past studies of the dangers of DDT usually focused on its environmental effects. Studies of DDT and human health have not considered the risks of applying it in high doses where humans may come into direct contact with the pesticide. DDT has its uses as a malarial preventative, the viewpoint authors admit, but it should be a last resort after other, less toxic measures have been attempted, concluding that when DDT must be used, careful oversight by authorities is needed.*

A panel of experts and citizens convened to review recent studies on the link between DDT and human health expressed concern that the current practice of spraying the pesticide indoors to fight malaria is leading to unprecedented— and insufficiently monitored—levels of exposure to it.

## A Call for Reduced Exposure to DDT

Although DDT has been largely abandoned as an agricultural pesticide worldwide, its use to combat malaria was endorsed in 2006 by the World Health Organization (WHO) and by officials in the President's Malaria Initiative, a program led by the U.S. Agency for International Development, which was launched by former President George W. Bush in 2005. According to WHO, in 2006 alone there were 247 million cases of and 880,000 deaths from malaria. Most of the deaths were of young children in Africa.

In regions where malaria is endemic, the organochlorine pesticide (i.e., DDT) is now sprayed inside buildings and homes to repel and kill the mosquitoes that spread the disease. This is being done despite a paucity of data on the human health impacts of DDT exposure at such high levels in currently exposed populations, according to the experts from fields ranging from environmental health to cancer biology.

After a review of nearly 500 epidemiological studies, . . . published online Monday, May 4, [2009] ahead of print in the journal Environmental Health Perspectives, the researchers developed a consensus statement calling for increased efforts to reduce exposure to DDT, to understand the health effects of exposure to DDT, and to develop alternatives to using DDT so that other methods could ultimately be relied upon for malaria control.

Examples of non-chemical measures to control malaria include the use of bed nets, draining sources of standing water or filling them up with soil, and the rapid diagnosis and treatment of malaria cases.

## Studies on Human Health and DDT Are Limited

"We have to put our concerns in the context of people dying of malaria," said lead author Brenda Eskenazi, UC Berkeley professor of epidemiology and of maternal and child health at the School of Public Health. "We know DDT can save lives by repelling and killing disease-spreading mosquitoes. But evidence suggests that people living in areas where DDT is used are exposed to very high levels of the pesticide. The only published studies on health effects conducted in these populations have shown profound effects on male fertility. Clearly, more research is needed on the health of populations where indoor residual spraying is occurring, but in the meantime, DDT should really be the last resort against malaria rather than the first line of defense."

The researchers noted that the majority of studies on DDT have focused on the impact on wildlife and the environment. Of the studies published on human health, almost all have dealt with populations exposed to low, background levels of DDT. Nevertheless, some of those studies have suggested links between DDT and cancer risk, diabetes, developmental problems in fetuses and in children, and decreased fertility.

"Any studies conducted up to now on the human health effects from DDT exposure may not be relevant to the populations currently exposed to the pesticide through indoor residual spraying," said Eskenazi, who has published research on the negative impact of DDT exposure to a child's neurodevelopment.

Moreover, most of the studies on DDT and human health were done in developed countries where the pesticide was banned in the 1970s, the researchers said.

## Ineffective Oversight

"DDT is now used in countries where many of the people are malnourished, extremely poor and possibly suffering from immune-compromising diseases such as AIDS, which may increase their susceptibility to chemical exposures," said co-author Jonathan Chevrier, UC Berkeley post-doctoral researcher in epidemiology and in environmental health sciences.

DDT has been banned in the United States since 1972. To date, more than 160 countries have signed the Stockholm Convention on Persistent Organic Pollutants, an international treaty banning DDT and 11 other persistent organic pollutants, except when needed for malaria control.

In cases where DDT must be used, the Stockholm Convention requires an implementation and management plan to minimize the pesticide's exposure to humans and its release into the environment. However, the authors noted, little oversight exists to ensure that those plans are being carried out properly.

"There are anecdotal reports of people failing to remove their clothes and cooking utensils from their homes before DDT spraying," said Chevrier. "More training and monitoring is needed to prevent such instances."

## A Consensus Statement

The consensus statement emerged from a March 2008 conference jointly organized by the Pine River Superfund Citizen Task Force, the Center for Responsible Leadership and the Public Affairs Institute of Alma College. More than 200 participants attended the conference, which was held near the site in St. Louis, Mich., where a chemical plant [leaked] massive levels of DDT into Pine River. In 1983, the area was named a Superfund site [an area contaminated by hazardous substances] by the U.S. Environmental Protection Agency.

# National Security and Environmentalism Must Work Collaboratively

*Gal Luft*

*Gal Luft is executive director of the Institute for the Analysis of Global Security and cofounder of the Set America Free Coalition. He is coauthor of* Energy Security Challenges in the 21st Century *and* Turning Oil into Salt: Energy Independence Through Fuel Choice.

*In the following viewpoint, Luft maintains that though green activists (conservationists) and security hawks (those concerned with keeping America safe) would seem to have a similar desire to curtail American dependency on foreign oil, reality often finds these two groups at odds with each other. Yet Luft contends that despite differences between those on the American political right and those on the left, a middle ground needs to be found that will be acceptable to both camps. For greens, the enemy is carbon emissions, which encompass a broad spectrum of energy concerns; hawks focus more narrowly on transportation's dependence on oil. Luft suggests that first, both groups can agree that an economically strong America serves their interests. Second, he would concentrate energy policy on developing electrically powered cars and trucks to reduce America's need to fund "rogue states" in the Middle East.*

Many Americans perceive the fight for energy security and the effort to reduce our oil dependence as synonymous with the effort to curb greenhouse gas emissions. Politicians talking about energy often bind together energy security and the environment, creating the impression that using less oil

Gal Luft, "Greens & Hawks: An Uneasy Alliance," *inFOCUS Quarterly*, Fall 2009, pp. 11–13. Reproduced by permission.

would not only slow down the transfer of wealth to oil-exporting regimes, but also the melting of the icecaps.

To some degree this is true. Many components of energy policy, like increased fuel efficiency, the use of mass transit, the shift to some renewable fuels, and the electrification of transportation, can offer both security and environmental benefits. If a car uses less gasoline, fewer dollars migrate abroad, and fewer tons of carbon dioxide release into the atmosphere.

Greens and hawks have much to agree on in pursuing their respective goals. But these two constituencies are not as aligned as many tend to think. Energy security and greenhouse gas reduction are not complementary issues. Many of the technologies and policies that could assist one could well be an impediment to the other.

## Mapping the Interests

Let's begin with environmentalists. In the short history of the 21st century, no issue has risen from near obscurity to the center of our public discourse as quickly as global warming. What started as chatter among some concerned scientists and die-hard environmentalists is now called "the challenge of our generation," consuming a bandwidth equivalent of war among world leaders.

For environmentalists, the enemy is carbon. They measure every source of energy by its carbon content, and every human activity by its carbon footprint. Accordingly, carbon-emitting fossil fuels like coal, oil, and natural gas are viewed with scorn.

On the other side, there are the security hawks. As they see it, green may be the color of environmentalism, but it is also the color of the flag of the Islamists who wish us dead. They also note that green is the color of our currency, the dollar, which is in grave danger as a result of our economic decline, the mounting national debt, and our growing trade deficit, largely caused by our thirst for oil imports.

These concerns have lured conservatives, evangelical Christians, veterans, and Jews into the energy debate. For them, national security and economic security are a higher priority than global warming. They see the energy challenge in the context of the war on radical Islam. We are dependent on those who wish us ill, and who are using our petrodollars against us. Indeed, more than three-quarters of the world's oil reserves are in countries where radical Islam is on the rise.

Hawks are traditionally interested in reforming the transportation sector, 95 percent of which is powered by petroleum. By contrast, environmentalists are concerned with a broader set of issues, including electricity generation and transmission. However, contrary to popular thinking, America hardly generates any electricity from oil. Indeed, much has changed since the 1970s, when we generated a significant percentage of our electricity from oil, which made conserving electricity tantamount to saving oil. Today only 2 percent of our power is generated from oil.

Thus, despite claims that nuclear energy, solar, and wind power can reduce oil use, such sources of energy are irrelevant to breaking our oil dependence. If we build more nuclear reactors, solar panels, or wind farms, we might displace coal or natural gas. However, there will be virtually no oil displacement.

## Between Energy and Environment

Perhaps the biggest bone of contention between greens and conservatives in the U.S. has to do with the utilization of domestic energy resources. Hawks seek to tap energy resources in the U.S. in order to reduce our reliance on foreign sources. Greens are steadfastly opposed.

According to the U.S. Department of Interior, there are 21 billion barrels of conventional crude oil and 187 trillion cubic feet of natural gas below federally-controlled lands, mostly in the Western U.S. and in Alaska. An additional 85 billion barrels are believed to lie offshore, in the Outer Continental Shelf of the U.S. (To put these figures in perspective, U.S. annual oil consumption in 2007 stood at 7.5 billion barrels and its natural gas consumption stood at 23 trillion cubic feet.) However, environmental opposition has put these resources mostly out of reach.

Similarly, environmental opposition has blocked non-conventional sources of crude. With 25 percent of the world's coal reserves, the U.S. could deploy coal-to-liquids technology, which would be profitable as long as crude oil remains above $60 a barrel. But, for environmentalists, using coal to displace oil is a nightmare scenario. Indeed, coal-derived fuel produces twice as much $CO_2$ per unit as petroleum-based fuel.

Other non-conventional oils like oil shale and Canadian tar sands are equally problematic for greens.

Biofuels also pose a challenge to many environmentalists. Rising global demand for biofuels has caused Indonesia, where palm-oil plantations are grown for biodiesel production, to clear land for new crops, thereby removing $CO_2$-soaking forests. This now makes Indonesia the world's third largest emitter, after the U.S. and China.

Broadly speaking, many environmentalists who in the past strongly supported biofuels now oppose them because of the unintended consequences of the sudden growth of the industry, which they view as unsustainable. Security hawks, by contrast, see biofuels as an immediate and imperative oil displacement strategy.

If there is an inconvenient truth, it may be that we are thus far unable to address the concerns of both camps simultaneously.

## A Tale of Two Presidents

During the eight years of the George W. Bush Administration, the U.S. faced constant reminders of its energy security challenge. This included geopolitical tensions with oil exporters, hurricanes in the Gulf of Mexico, the rise of China, and a seven-fold increase in the price of crude oil. Accordingly, energy security assumed a far higher priority than global warming; Bush pushed for increased domestic oil production, investment in the development of shale oil, and a streamlined refinery permitting process.

Since stating in his State of the Union address that, "America is addicted to oil," Bush became increasingly open to policies anathema to many conservatives. The Energy Independence and Security Act of 2007 raised the Corporate Average Fuel Economy (CAFE) standard for the first time since 1978, setting a target of 35 miles per gallon (mpg) for cars and light trucks by 2020. The law also set a mandatory Renewable Fuel Standard (RFS), requiring fuel producers to use at least 36 billion gallons of biofuels (mostly made from non-food crops) in 2022—nearly five times the current levels.

While these policies sat well with environmentalists, the Bush Administration's overall indifference to global warming and its rejection of international pressure to adopt restrictions on greenhouse gas emissions infuriated the movement.

The Barack Obama Administration and the Democrat-controlled 111th Congress have since made sweeping changes. Even before entering the White House, President Obama declared his commitment to take aggressive measures to reduce carbon dioxide emissions by 80 percent by 2050, and to sign up America for a post-Kyoto international regime to combat global warming.

Obama also pledged to end America's oil dependence. As the Democratic presidential nominee, he said: "I will set a clear goal as president: In 10 years we will finally end our dependence on oil in the Middle East." Once elected, he imple-

mented oil policies that are in sync with environmental principles. The most significant was his increase in fuel efficiency
standards. In May 2009, he announced new CAFE standards
of 35.5 mpg by 2016.

When faced with tradeoffs between security and the environment, Obama has been more green than hawk. His Environmental Protection Agency, for example, seeks to penalize
farmers for cutting down trees or switching crops to grow
corn for ethanol. The policy is clear: Regardless of how many
petrodollars it diverts from dangerous regimes, ethanol is only
acceptable as an alternative fuel if its carbon footprint is low.

The first energy legislation passed by the House of Representatives during the Obama Administration, the American
Clean Energy and Security Act of 2009 (also known as the
Waxman-Markey cap-and-trade bill), takes ambitious measures to reduce greenhouse gas emissions. However, despite
claims that the bill will reduce America's oil dependence, the
legislation would do little in that regard. In fact, by penalizing
coal more harshly than oil due to its higher carbon content,
the bill might actually increase oil use for electricity generation.

Global warming also appears to trump security in Obama's
foreign policy. Consider the case of India, where growing demand for electricity poses a dilemma. As the owner of 10 percent of the world's coal reserves, India could provide for most
of its own power needs. However, environmentalists warn that
coal power for one billion Indians means a lot of $CO_2$. By
contrast, security-minded people are more concerned about
India shifting to the cleaner alternative, natural gas. Should
India decide to power its turbines with natural gas, it is likely
to become increasingly dependent on neighboring Iran, the
world's second largest natural gas reserve.

In May 2009, Iran and Pakistan signed a deal to connect
their economies via a 1,300-mile natural gas pipeline. Iran is
eager to extend the pipeline to India. Access to the Indian

*A worker assembles the engine of a commercial zero-emission plug-in truck at the Smith Electric Vehicles production facility in Kansas City, Missouri, USA, on November 17, 2010. Gal Luft argues that both conservationists and 'security hawks' can be appeased by reducing dependence on foreign sources of oil through the use of electric vehicles.* © Patrick Fallon/ Bloomberg via Getty Images.

subcontinent means an economic lifeline, particularly at a time when the U.S. is trying to weaken it economically with sanctions. The Bush Administration was vocally opposed to the pipeline project, and offered India civilian nuclear assistance as a way to scale up electricity production. The Obama Administration, by contrast, has been mute on the issue. Instead, it has pressured India to give more consideration to global warming.

In a July 2009 visit in India, Secretary of State Hillary Clinton urged New Delhi to accept binding limits on carbon emissions. The Indian people, on a per capita basis, have among the world's lowest emissions. They flatly rejected Clinton's proposal. But continuous pressure by the Obama Administration to reduce its emissions could bring India to change course and deal directly with Iran.

# Squaring Security and Environmental Concerns

What can greens and hawks agree on?

First, both must recognize that in order to address any of their goals, we must first prosper. If there is any hope for significant greenhouse gas reduction, it comes from wealthy industrial countries. The salvation certainly won't come from developing countries like China and India, where environmental concerns are a distant second to basic human needs—access to electricity, food, and shelter.

Therefore, curbing greenhouse gas emissions would be contingent on the prosperity and economic resilience of America and other developed nations. A weakened, economically depleted America doesn't bode well for the climate movement. Conversely, prosperity is difficult to achieve, as long as our economy hemorrhages money to purchase foreign oil.

Second, both greens and hawks must recognize that oil's strategic status derives not from the amount of oil we import or consume, but from its virtual monopoly over transportation fuel. As long as the vast majority of our cars and trucks can run on nothing but oil, alternatives to oil will be shut out of the transportation fuel market and we will forever be beholden to rogue states.

The key to both energy security and reduced carbon emissions is therefore in vehicle platforms that enable fuel competition. Existing technology, in the form of flexible fuel vehicles, is the answer. New cars sold in the U.S. that are equipped with an internal combustion engine should allow for fuel competition by being flexible fuel vehicles. Similarly, new diesel cars should be capable of operating on biodiesel. Such an open fuel standard would help to protect the U.S. economy from high and volatile oil prices and from the threats caused by global instability, while enabling market penetration of alternative fuels that are less carbon intensive.

And because electricity is 98 percent petroleum-free, greens and hawks can also work together to speed up the commercialization of electric cars and plug-in hybrids. This, too, would satisfy the concerns of the environmental movement, while bolstering national security.

In the end, greens and hawks must focus on a unified agenda. Without identifying commonalities, both will continue to undercut each other, leaving America exposed.

# For Further Discussion

1. Using viewpoints by Dianne Newell and Cheryll Glotfelty to inform your response, explain how Carson uses her writing skills, including her powers of description and rhetoric, to make a passionate argument against chemical agriculture.

2. How does *Silent Spring* go beyond the subject of chemical agriculture to argue for a new, balanced way of interacting with nature, according to viewpoints by Priscilla Coit Murphy, John Burnside, and Brian Bethune?

3. Many have interpreted *Silent Spring* as being completely against the spraying of pesticides. How does Carson acknowledge their usefulness and take a balanced approach to their use? Consult viewpoints by Priscilla Coit Murphy, John Burnside, Rachel Carson, and Brian Bethune to help formulate your response.

4. According to viewpoints by Terry Tempest Williams, Priscilla Coit Murphy, Marla Cone, and Colin Tudge, in what ways can *Silent Spring* be viewed as having jump-started the modern environmental movement?

5. Should human beings live in harmony with nature, taking a balanced view of the environment, as advocated by David R. Loy, or should nature be at the disposal of human beings, to do with as desired, as Wesley J. Smith and James Delingpole assert?

6. Is *Silent Spring* truly one of the books that has changed the course of history, such as Harriet Beecher Stowe's *Uncle Tom's Cabin* and Charles Darwin's *The Origin of Species*, or is it something less? Consult viewpoints by Priscilla Coit Murphy, Ronald Bailey, and Brian Bethune to support your conclusion.

7. Carson has been accused of contributing to the death of millions of African babies from malaria because DDT was banned following the publication of *Silent Spring.* Is this a valid argument? How do the viewpoints by Ronald Bailey, Brian Bethune, and the health editors at NewsRx support or challenge this argument?

# For Further Reading

Edward Abbey, *Down the River*. New York: Dutton, 1982.

———, *The Monkey Wrench Gang*. Philadelphia: Lippincott, 1975.

T.C. Boyle, *A Friend of the Earth*. New York: Viking, 2000.

Rachel Carson, *The Edge of the Sea*. Boston: Houghton Mifflin, 1955.

———, *The Sea Around Us*. New York: Oxford University Press, 1951.

———, *Under the Sea-Wind*. New York: Oxford University Press, 1941.

Annie Dillard, *Pilgrim at Tinker Creek*. New York: Harper's Magazine Press, 1974.

Albert Gore, *An Inconvenient Truth: The Planetary Emergency of Global Warming and What We Can Do About It*. New York: Rodale Press, 2006.

Jon Krakauer, *Into the Wild*. New York: Villard Books, 1996.

Aldo Leopold, *A Sand County Almanac, and Sketches Here and There*. New York: Oxford University Press, 1987.

Bill McKibben, *The Bill McKibben Reader: Pieces from an Active Life*. New York: Henry Holt, 2008.

Henry David Thoreau, *The Natural History Essays*. Salt Lake City: Peregrine Smith, 1980.

———, *Walden*. Boston: Ticknor and Fields, 1842.

Terry Tempest Williams, *Refuge: An Unnatural History of Family and Place*. New York: Pantheon, 1991.

# Bibliography

## Books

Paul Brooks

*Speaking for Nature: How Literary Naturalists from Henry Thoreau to Rachel Carson Have Shaped America.* Boston: Houghton Mifflin, 1980.

Paul Brooks and Rachel Carson

*The House of Life: Rachel Carson at Work.* Boston: Houghton Mifflin, 1972.

Rachel Carson, Dorothy Freeman, and Martha E. Freeman

*Always, Rachel: The Letters of Rachel Carson and Dorothy Freeman, 1952–1964.* Boston: Beacon Press, 1995.

Barbara J. Cook

*Women Writing Nature: A Feminist View.* Lanham, MD: Lexington Books, 2008.

Jeff Crane and Michael Egan

*Natural Protest: Essays on the History of American Environmentalism.* New York: Routledge, 2009.

Riley E. Dunlap and Angela G. Mertig

*American Environmentalism: The U.S. Environmental Movement, 1970–1990.* Philadelphia: Taylor & Francis, 1992.

Thomas R. Dunlap

*DDT, "Silent Spring," and the Rise of Environmentalism: Classic Texts.* Seattle: University of Washington Press, 2008.

Frank Graham

*Since "Silent Spring."* Boston: Houghton Mifflin, 1970.

| H.P. Hynes | *The Recurring Silent Spring.* New York: Pergamon Press, 1989. |

Linda J. Lear — *Rachel Carson: Witness for Nature.* New York: H. Holt, 1997.

Ellen Levin — *Rachel Carson: A Twentieth-Century Life.* New York: Viking, 2007.

Mark H. Lytle — *The Gentle Subversive: Rachel Carson, "Silent Spring," and the Rise of the Environmental Movement.* New York: Oxford University Press, 2007.

Alex MacGillivray — *Rachel Carson's "Silent Spring."* Hauppauge, NY: Barron's, 2004.

Gino J. Marco, Robert M. Hollingworth, William Durham, and Rachel Carson — *Silent Spring Revisited.* Washington, DC: American Chemical Society, 1987.

Peter Matthiessen — *Courage for the Earth: Writers, Scientists, and Activists Celebrate the Life and Writing of Rachel Carson.* Boston: Houghton Mifflin, 2007.

Mary A. McCay — *Rachel Carson.* New York: Twayne Publishers, 1993.

Bill McKibben and Albert Gore — *American Earth: Environmental Writing Since Thoreau.* New York: Literary Classics of the United States, 2008.

David Michaels            *Doubt Is Their Product: How
                          Industry's Assault on Science
                          Threatens Your Health.* Oxford:
                          Oxford University Press, 2008.

Naomi Oreskes             *Merchants of Doubt: How a Handful
and Erik M.               of Scientists Obscured the Truth on
Conway                    Issues from Tobacco Smoke to Global
                          Warming.* New York: Bloomsbury
                          Press, 2010.

Arlene R.                 *Rachel Carson: A Biography.*
Quaratiello               Westport, CT: Greenwood Press,
                          2004.

Edmund Russell            *War and Nature: Fighting Humans
                          and Insects with Chemicals from
                          World War I to "Silent Spring."*
                          Cambridge: Cambridge University
                          Press, 2001.

Lisa H. Sideris           *Rachel Carson: Legacy and Challenge.*
and Kathleen D.           Albany: State University of New York
Moore                     Press, 2008.

Philip Sterling           *Sea and Earth: The Life of Rachel
                          Carson.* New York: Crowell, 1970.

Edward O. Wilson          *The Creation: An Appeal to Save Life
                          on Earth.* New York: Norton, 2006.

## Periodicals and Internet Sources

David Ackerson            "From Romanticism to Deep
                          Ecology: The Continuing Evolution
                          in American Environmental
                          Thought," *Taproot,* vol. 12, no. 3,
                          2000.

Philip Cafaro        "Features—Thoreau, Leopold, and
                     Carson: Toward an Environmental
                     Virtue Ethics," *Environmental Ethics*,
                     vol. 23, no.1, 2001.

Yaakov Garb          "Rachel Carson's *Silent Spring*,"
                     *Dissent*, vol. 42, no. 4, 1995.

Maril Hazlett        "'Woman vs. Man vs. Bugs': Gender
                     and Popular Ecology in Early
                     Reactions to *Silent Spring*,"
                     *Environmental History*, vol. 9, no. 4,
                     2004.

William Howarth      "Turning the Tide—How Rachel
                     Carson Became a Woman of Letters,"
                     *American Scholar*, vol. 74, no. 3,
                     2005.

Reed Karaim          "Not So Fast with the DDT—Rachel
                     Carson's Warnings Still Apply,"
                     *American Scholar*, vol. 74, no. 3,
                     2005.

D.J. Kevles          "The Contested Earth: Science,
                     Equity & the Environment,"
                     *Daedalus*, vol. 137, no. 2, 2008.

Christina Larson     "Party Smashers: Washington Was
                     Supposed to Celebrate Rachel
                     Carson's 100th Birthday This Year.
                     Then the GOP Got the Invite,"
                     *Washington Monthly*, vol. 39, no. 10,
                     2007.

Iain Murray          "Silent Alarmism," *National Review
                     Online*, May 31, 2007.
                     www.nationalreview.com.

Laura Orlando "Industry Attacks on Dissent: From Rachel Carson to Oprah Forty Years After the Publication of *Silent Spring*, Corporations Are Still Trying to Silence Critics," *Dollars & Sense*, 2002.

Carl Pope "Trashing Rachel Carson," *Sierra*, September/October 2007.

John Tierney "Fateful Voice of a Generation Still Drowns Out Real Science," *New York Times*, June 5, 2007.

Martin J. Walker "The Unquiet Voice of *Silent Spring*: The Legacy of Rachel Carson," *Ecologist*, August/September 1999.

Bruce Watson "Presence of Mind: Sounding the Alarm—Rachel Carson Sparked a Movement with *Silent Spring*," *Smithsonian*, vol. 33, no. 6, 2002.

# Index

39 60